AROUND rome WITH KIDS

by Dana Prescott

Fodor's Travel Publications
New York • Toronto • London • Sydney • Auckland

www.fodors.com

CREDITS
Writer: Dana Prescott

Series Editors: Karen Cure, Andrea Lehman
Editor: Andrea Lehman
Editorial Production: Marina Padakis
Production/Manufacturing: Colleen Ziemba

Design: Fabrizio La Rocca, creative director; Tigist Getachew, art director
Illustration and Series Design: Rico Lins, Keren Ora Admoni/Rico Lins Studio
Additional Illustrations: Jacob Carroll

ABOUT THE WRITER

Dana Prescott first traveled to Rome when she was 19 years old. Half Italian, she is a painter, writer, and educator who has been living and working in Rome for most of the past 20 years.

ISBN 0–676–90188–3
ISSN 1557–5544
First Edition

IMPORTANT TIPS

Although all prices, opening times, and other details in this book are based on information supplied to us at press time, changes occur all the time in the travel world, and Fodor's cannot accept responsibility for facts that become outdated or for inadvertent errors or omissions. So always confirm information when it matters, especially if you're making a detour to visit a specific place.

SPECIAL SALES

Fodor's Travel Publications are available at special discounts for bulk purchases for sales promotions or premiums. Special editions, including personalized covers, excerpts of existing guides, and corporate imprints, can be created in large quantities for special needs. For more information, contact your local bookseller or Special Markets, Fodor's Travel Publications, 280 Park Avenue, New York, NY 10017. Inquiries from Canada should be directed to your local Canadian bookseller or sent to Random House of Canada, Ltd., Marketing Dept., 2775 Matheson Boulevard East, Mississauga, Ontario L4W 4P7. Inquiries from the United Kingdom should be sent to Fodor's Travel Publications, 20 Vauxhall Bridge Road, London, England SW1V 2SA.

PRINTED IN THE UNITED STATES OF AMERICA
10 9 8 7 6 5 4 3 2 1

COUNTDOWN TO GOOD TIMES

GET READY, GET SET!

WHEN IN ROME

Italians are famous for many things—their fabulous food, their friendliness, and their history, art, culture, and architecture. Rome, like Italy's other great cities, is a perfect family destination because all of the above are woven into the fabric of daily excursions and adventures. Add to that an enthusiastic welcome, like those that have greeted travelers here for centuries.

Though there isn't much in Rome geared especially for kids, children just love the Eternal City. You won't find many kid-specific attractions, kids' menus (order half portions of adult meals), or, frankly, much kid culture. You won't even find many public spaces designed for children's safety. (The city has very few sidewalks but lots of intense traffic, noise, and chaos, and playgrounds aren't particularly safety-conscious.) Still, Rome manages to make kids feel instantly a part of daily life. It's a place to rediscover simple pleasures as a family: lingering over meals, initiating conversations with strangers, sketching, people-watching, and really seeing things. A day spent in a piazza watching your children chase pigeons can be more memorable than visiting a famous museum. Do as the Romans do. Visit these 68 sights with the shared goal of family—not just kid—pleasure.

PLANNING A GREAT DAY

No matter your kids' ages or interests, there's a Roman treat for every appetite. History, art, people, and ideas, not to mention great food (even the fanciest restaurants welcome children), a mild climate, family-run businesses, and the Italian love for children create a perfect backdrop for your *soggiorno*. Slow down and set modest goals so you can digest what you see and keep everyone in good humor. Choose a few things to do each day. Make stops for ice cream, piazza-sitting, and *far niente* (doing nothing). And maintain a high threshold for frustration and ambiguity.

Leaf through this book and select sights of interest to your kids, but choose nearby backups in case your first choice is closed. The hours listed in this book represent regular non-holiday operating hours, but Roman sights are notoriously unpredictable. Purchase an Italian calendar, so you'll be forewarned about national holidays and saints' days (for example, all Rome closes down for St. Peter and St. Paul Day on June 29). Remember, too, that summer hours are often extended and that the occasional strike (*sciopero*) or meeting can close museums and monuments. Call before you go to confirm open hours, and use the neighborhood directory (All Around Town) and the thematic directory (Something for Everyone) at the back of this book to make contingency plans. And while you're flipping to the back of the book, check out the cool flip art in the lower right corner.

GETTING AROUND

Staying in the city center is ideal, because then you can see much of Rome by foot—best for seeing the little things. Fountains and *fontanelle* spray water. Hawks, gulls, pigeons, and swallows wheel lazily around church domes. A stroll reveals stone animals and other carving, patches of green, and street cats asleep in the sun. Remember, though, that Rome is a city of impatient and impetuous drivers, where traffic signals seem purely advisory. Stress street safety first and foremost with your kids.

Public transportation is another good choice. It's extensive, always expanding, but subject to occasional strikes and overcrowding. Get a good ATAC map with all the *linee urbane* city bus and metro routes outlined. Be forewarned that little access has been provided for the disabled, and even stroller access can be difficult.

MONEY MATTERS

Just as traffic signals are open to individual interpretation, museum discounts can be, too. Most museums list discounts for senior citizens, students, and children, but these discounts may not be applicable to you. Some museums and monuments honor discounts only for members of the European Community, with free admission guaranteed for EU visitors up to 18 and over 60. So plan on paying the full price listed in this book, but ask for children's and student discounts when you arrive.

A good money-saving option is a five-day combination ticket that lets you see the best of ancient Rome for a discounted price (€15.50). Attractions covered by the pass include the Colosseo, Palazzo Altemps, Palazzo Massimo alle Terme, Terme di Diocleziano, and others. Ask at the entrance to the first sight you visit. Another option is the Itinere card, which covers seven days' admission to 17 city museums for just €12.95. The card is available in some bookstores, some banks, most large travel agencies, and some hotels. Their web site (www.itinere.it) lists where to get them. To prebook tickets to many museums and archaeological sites in English, contact Pierreci (tel. 06/39.96.77.00, www.pierreci.it).

HANG OUT AT BARS

Yes, I'm serious. Most bars have telephones and bathrooms, hard and soft drinks, ice cream, sandwiches, takeout, advice, and humor. *Baristi* (bartenders) can even help you navigate the neighborhood. It's enough to frequent their bar for coffee a few mornings in a row, and they will happily help you out. One rung up the eating-place ladder is the *tavola calda,* which usually serves a few hot dishes along with sandwiches. Though you can sit down to eat, you won't get the full service of a restaurant. Speaking of restaurants, Italian restaurants don't tend to serve breakfast (only bars do), because Italians don't generally eat a hearty, American-style breakfast.

RESOURCES AND INFORMATION

In Rome for a prolonged stay? Join the public kids' library system, not only for the pleasure of borrowing books, but for talks, authors' readings, illustrators' workshops, and discounts at hip stores with a library card. Subscribe to *Wanted in Rome,* the English weekly with everything from art reviews to apartment sublets.

Useful web sites include www.inforoma.it, the city's official tourism site; www.beniculturali. it/cartine-html/lazio.html, the official site for the cultural ministry, listing most museums and hours; www.comune.roma.it, with all city museums and schedules; and www. romace.it, which contains a weekly publication called *Roma C'è,* which outlines exhibits, theatrical events, musical performances, and workshops. You can purchase hard copy at newsstands on Thursdays; look for the section in English in the back.

Tourist Information Points (PIT) dot the city and are open daily 9–6. If the sight you are interested in visiting has no phone number, the number of the closest PIT is listed in this book. For other information, contact the Rome Tourist Board (tel. 06/48.89.92.55), whose staff speaks several languages. It's open Monday–Friday 8:15–7:15 and Saturday 7:15–1:45.

Be prepared for Italians to provide unsolicited parenting advice, too. They hate to see kids barefoot at any age, believe strongly that *corrente* (wind) is an enemy of children's health, and that a safe environment is something you must provide for your child rather than expect the city to. Take these suggestions as an opportunity for interaction, one of the most enjoyable aspects of a visit to Rome.

Lots of moms and dads were interviewed to create these suggestions, and we'd love to add yours. E-mail us your kid-friendly additions at editors@fodors.com (specify Around Rome with Kids on the subject line), or write to us at Around Rome with Kids, Fodor's Travel Publications, 280 Park Avenue, New York, NY 10017.

NOW GO
And go and go. Like all truly great cities, Rome grows with you and your children. Throw those coins in the Fontana di Trevi, and come back again and again. Rome will never cease to nourish your family's interests, enthusiasm, and daily lives.

— Dana Prescott

ALTARE DELLA PATRIA

Michael Jackson asked for one thing when he came to Rome—to climb the Altare della Patria (Altar of the Nation). Called by some the Typewriter or the Wedding Cake, the monument was built by Guiseppe Sacconi at the turn of the last century in honor of united Italy's first king: Victor Emmanuel II. This landmark that so fascinated the King of Pop is the source of great debate, love or hate, on the part of Italians. Is it beautiful? Ugly? You decide.

Immense, white, and startling in its placement next to the church of Santa Maria in Ara Coeli, the monument provides beautiful views of Rome and an exquisite composition of intersecting staircases, perfect for a dash to the top. The first 47 steps lead you to the tomb of the unknown soldier, guarded by armed police officers. Another 85 steps bring you to the base of the immense equestrian statue of Victor Emmanuel himself. After an additional 49 steps, you arrive at the first large piazza, from which you can see the Pantheon (*see* #25), the Torre di Miliza, and all of Via del Corso. Buses begin to look the size of

KEEP IN MIND The war buff in your family will not want to miss the tiny but fascinating museum housed under the monument's staircase. (Turn left as you face the monument and enter at the second doorway.) The recently reopened Museo Centrale del Risorgimento contains a collection of war memorabilia, offers a cool respite from the heat, and is free. It's open Tuesday–Sunday 10–6.

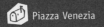 Piazza Venezia

  Free

 06/58.89.51

Daily 10–5, weather permitting

4 and up

Matchbox cars from this level. Another 22 stairs take you to the next city overlook, and 34 more place you under the marble columns of the loggia. Surrounded by shade and cool, you can climb the final seven steps (grand total: 244) and look up at the beautifully decorated ceilings covered with mosaics and frescoes. Through each doorway and set of columns, spectacular views reveal themselves.

Take your time. Each overlook is a photo op. Check out the plantings in the piazza's traffic circle, which change with each season. In the distance you can see the Castelli Romani, the hill of Montemario, and the dome of San Pietro. Look for the Pantheon's roof and the twisting spiral of Sant'Ivo's church, by Borromini. The views of the Palatino and Castel Sant'Angelo, San Giovanni in Laterano, and the Colosseo are spectacular.

HEY, KIDS! If you get here at opening or closing time, you'll witness the immense iron gate rising slowly out of the sidewalk or sinking dramatically back in. It looks too huge to move, but it does. So try to be the first in or the last out. It's fun.

EATS FOR KIDS Before or after your visit, hit **Gelateria Artigiana Yogurteria Ara Coeli** (Piazza d'Ara Coeli 9/10, tel. 06/79.50.85), where favorite ice cream flavors include mango, kiwi, gourmet coffee, and chocolate chip. If the weather is good, book an outside table at **Vecchia Roma** (Piazza Campitelli 18, tel. 06/68.64.60) or **La Taverna degli Amici** (Piazza Tormargana 36/37, tel. 06/69.20.04.93). Both are great restaurants in elegant little piazza settings.

ARCHEOBUS

67

I f you want to see many of Rome's major sights without worrying about parking or hailing cabs, the Archeobus, a new city bus service, may be for you. Leaving every hour on the hour from in front of the church of San Marco, the 16-seat bus follows a loop with 21 stops. Your ticket permits you to get on and off as you wish. If you stay on the bus without getting off at all, the entire loop takes about two hours. If instead you decide to get off at sights of interest, the trip may take all day. When you're done at each sight, you simply board the next Archeobus and continue the circuit.

Other nice things about this bus service include an extremely reasonable cost and good visibility. Though buses are small, you ride up high. The route hits most of the major ancient sights you would want to see—the Bocca della Verità (see #63), Circo Massimo, Terme di Caracalla (Baths of Caracalla), Museo delle Mura di Roma (see #38), the catacombs, Via Appia Antica (see #8), and a stretch of aqueducts—all in one fell swoop.

EATS FOR KIDS Many sights along the way, including the Bocca della Verità and Via Appia Antica have good restaurants nearby (see specific listings). But whatever your lunch plans, be sure to pack a light snack and some water bottles for the bus ride itself.

KEEP IN MIND You can prebook your seats via the Internet. Just look for the information about reservations, and send an e-mail with the number of places you want, the date, and the time of departure. Alternatively, you can wait until the last minute and buy tickets on board from the hostess or driver, but you run the risk that the bus might be full. The most booked buses are those in late morning (10 and 11), but the worst thing that could happen is that the bus you were hoping for is filled and you have a coffee while waiting for the next one.

In front of San Marco, Piazza Venezia

 €7.75

 Daily 9–7

 06/46.95.46.95;
www.romavision.it/archeobus.htm

All ages

On board, an English-speaking hostess gives a brief overview of each stop, telling interesting facts about the art and history of each place to tempt you off the bus. Mercifully, the chatter is not nonstop. Each rider also receives an illustrated brochure (in English or Italian) of the route and points of interest.

The Archeobus is an ideal way to see the city's ancient sights with kids in tow. If your youngsters run out of steam, you can ride the bus back to Piazza Venezia. If they're still going strong, you can continue getting out at sights that interest you. Best of all, you can beat the heat, as all the buses are air-conditioned, a rarity in Rome, where many believe air-conditioning is bad for your health.

HEY, KIDS! You've heard the phrase "King of the Road?" The Archeobus takes you down the "Queen of the Roads": the Regina Viarum, the first building project of the great Roman roadway system. Some southern stretches of this road (beyond the reach of the Archeobus tour) were lined with canals, so travelers could get off their horses or out of carriages and take a boat ride instead. Imagine how much slower travel was in Roman times. A trip of 130 miles, for instance, would take five or six days. That's a trip your Archeobus could drive in just about three hours.

AUTOBUS 116

E ver hear of trying to get a camel through the eye of a needle? That's what it's like to drive a bus through the heart of ancient Rome. To address this problem, Rome's transport system has recently added a fleet of tiny electric buses and highly skilled *autiste* (drivers) to steer them.

Each little bright orange bus seats eight people, but many more passengers mount and stand while riding, holding onto metal bars and straps. The drivers are specially trained for maneuvering down winding streets lined with double-parked cars and motorcycles. Passengers sit enthralled and amazed as drivers slide past vehicles and buildings with only inches (sometimes less!) to spare.

A favorite of all the new electric bus routes is the 116, which begins on Via Veneto by the Villa Borghese (*see* #6), which you will also want to visit, and winds its way down through

EATS FOR KIDS You can get off anywhere to grab something to eat and reboard with the same ticket, as long as you're within the 90-minute limit. If hunger hits near the Pantheon, get an outside table at the restaurant **Santo Eustachio** (Piazza dei Caprettari 63, tel. 06/686.16.16). The *fritto vegetariano* (deep-fried cheese and vegetable platter), a specialty, is similar to tempura. Two world-famous *gelaterie* (ice cream shops) are also by the Pantheon: **Giolitti** (Via degli Uffici del Vicario 40, tel. 06/699.12.43) and **Della Palma** (Via della Maddalena 20/23, tel. 06/68.80.67.52). See if you can resist.

the densely parked and populated center of the city. It even drives within the shadow of the Pantheon, where no private cars are permitted.

Jump on the bus at its *capolinea* (head of the line) to be sure you get a seat for everyone in the family. Then stay on for the full round-trip; the bus retraces its route in only a few corners. Your ticket is good for 90 minutes, which will get you around the entire route and back to your starting point with time to spare.

While marveling as the driver passes cars and pedestrians with no room for error, you'll get a sense of the geography of the center of the city and its monuments as well as an up-close view of Rome without leaving your seat. If you prefer, you can jump off the bus if something interests you and board again using the same ticket, provided 90 minutes have not passed.

KEEP IN MIND
These minibuses often get crowded. Keep an eye on your wallet and other personal belongings when the bus begins to fill—another good reason to board at the capolinea, where you'll be guaranteed a seat.

HEY, KIDS! Though it may look like buses are free, they aren't. There's an honor system. To buy tickets (under $1 each), stop at a *tabbacio* (smoke shop, marked by a black sign with a white "T") or newsstand and ask (or have your parents ask) for *biglietti per l'autobus*. Once on board, look for the orange or yellow metal box, usually on a pole. Feed your ticket into the slot, and it'll be stamped with the date, time, and bus code. Then keep your ticket handy. Occasionally inspectors board buses to check that passengers have paid. Those who haven't get a heavy fine.

L'AVENTINO

65

Rome is famous for its seven hills. Of these, the Aventino (Aventine Hill) is most like an island unto itself. Come on a Sunday morning, when it is at its sleepiest. Few cars will interrupt your strolling, and you may very well intercept a wedding party or two at one of the churches. With a leisurely morning, you can cover everything listed here, all within walking distance.

Start in the small, intimate, and beautiful Parco Savelli. Below you, the Tevere and city rest quietly. When the kids get tired of hanging out in the park, head to the Piazza dei Cavalieri di Malta and Piranesi's church of Santa Maria del Priorato. It's the only architecture designed by Piranesi, the famed printmaker. But the piazza's real surprise for children (who need to be old enough to squint) is the keyhole in the doorway next to the church. As you squint, a beautiful view of Rome comes into focus. You can see a verdant adjoining garden, a tree-lined walkway, and beyond that, all the way to the white dome of San Pietro (St.

EATS FOR KIDS One of the hill's best restaurants is **Al Callarello** (Via Salvator Rosa 8, tel. 06/574.75.75). In good weather you can eat outside on the piazza. Leaving the Aventino heading towards Testaccio, you'll find **Perilli** (Via Marmorata 39, tel. 06/574.24.15), serving traditional Roman cooking.

KEEP IN MIND Older kids interested in music who can sit quietly for an hour might enjoy the evening vespers sung on Sunday at 7:15 in the Aventino's church of San Anselmo. About 50 monks sing, and the church bells are rung, creating an evocative close to the day. If everyone has had it with churches and needs a mega-dose of nature instead, head to the public rose garden, the Roseto Comunale (Via di Valle Murcia 6, tel. 06/574.68.10), which has thousands of varieties of roses. Bordering the Aventino, it is open May and June from 8 to 7 and is free.

Lungotevere Aventino to Via Marmarata, Viale
Gelsimini to Viale Aventino to Circo Massimo

Free

Daily 24 hrs

06/48.89.92.53 Rome Tourist Board

6 and up

Peter's), on the other side of the Tevere and a good mile or two north. In fact, you can see
two countries at once: the Vatican and Italy. Kids find great joy in seeing something so immense
through something so small. In springtime, the scent of orange trees makes the experience
of looking through the world's most famous keyhole even more magical.

Don't miss the church of Santa Sabina, just steps away in Piazza Pietro d'Illiria. The doors
of this church, made of cypress wood, depict scenes from both the Old and New testaments
that your kids will probably recognize. This is one of Rome's oldest churches, and its simplicity
is exhilarating. Even kids are relieved at the lack of ornamentation—just 24 enormous
Corinthian columns to consider.

You'll find no shops on the Aventino, just lovely old homes, gardens, walkways, piazzas,
churches, and a peaceful slice of Rome.

HEY, KIDS! Photographs of San Pietro through the keyhole are some
of the most famous pictures you'll find of Rome. But getting the shot of this
optical illusion isn't so easy. Try these approaches: Hold the camera right
against the keyhole and shoot. Then hold the camera back about an inch and
shoot again. Now try it from about a foot away. Which photo comes out better and why?

BAMBINO GESÙ

Do you believe in miracles? Bambino Gesù (Baby Jesus) is perhaps the most famous sacred image of Rome. Housed in a glass case in the church of Santa Maria in Ara Coeli, this relic is dressed in silk, wears chains of gold and pearls, and most important, has the power to cure the sick. He has even been known to revive the dead.

The original statue of Bambino Gesù was carved from a branch of an olive tree from the garden of Gethsemane. Stolen in 1994, the original baby was replaced by an exact copy, which has the same miraculous powers as the original. One of the most famous Bambino Gesù stories is that he once interrupted a speech Mussolini was giving in the adjoining piazza. Having been summoned to the bedside of a sick child, the doll was in a taxi that had to drive through the piazza right when Mussolini was talking. Even Il Duce couldn't stop him.

KEEP IN MIND While you're here, you'll want to visit the rest of the Campidoglio (see #62), but don't rush through the church after seeing Bambino Gesù. The church has wonderful frescoes by Pinturicchio (first chapel on the right), a lovely painted wooden ceiling, gorgeous ancient columns, and Murano glass chandeliers. Vito Macrit, the kind English-speaking volunteer who runs the gift shop next to Bambino Gesù's chapel, sells fragments of the baby's dress (sealed into key chains), rosaries, miniatures of the baby, and guidebooks on the church and its artworks.

Santa Maria in Ara Coeli,
Piazza Ara Coeli

 Free

Daily 6:30–6

 06/679.81.55

5 and up

To see how far Bambino Gesù's fame has spread, look at the baskets of mail from all over the world surrounding his house. Periodically the letters are collected and burned so the smoke will carry the letters' messages directly to the ears of God.

If you are in Rome on Christmas Eve, try to get to the Ara Coeli for Christmas Eve mass. Franciscan priests carry Bambino Gesù to the nativity scene near the front of the church, and, since touching the statue brings good luck, mobs flock here in hopes of touching the baby that evening. Gypsies especially turn out in all their finery for this tradition, which resembles a sacred football game. For a quieter celebration that still lets you see Bambino Gesù in action, come on Epiphany, when the figurine goes outside to bless Rome to the north, south, east, and west. But even if you aren't in Rome for the holidays, be sure to visit the world's most famous and powerful doll.

EATS FOR KIDS

Piazza Venezia has plenty of bars and a small grocery store, but for a sit-down meal, head to family-run **Da Giggetto** (see Carcere Mamertino), in the old Jewish Ghetto, or **Evangelista** (Via delle Zoccolette 11, tel. 06/ 687.58.10). See also Campidoglio.

HEY, KIDS! Not all tombs in all churches are hundreds of years old. For instance, check out the more recent tomb of a certain Prince Ruspoli. As you face the altar, it is on the left. The inscription tells us that the prince was an "ardent explorer of Africa." At the age of 27, he was killed by an infuriated elephant, but though he died in 1891, his body wasn't returned to Rome for burial until 1928. There's even a map carved in marble outlining precisely where his death occurred.

BOCCA DELLA VERITÀ

I n today's courts, witnesses swear to tell "the truth, the whole truth, and nothing but the truth," but in Roman times, things were different for people being questioned. Long before the advent of lie-detector machines, and even before there were bibles to swear on, there was the Bocca della Verità (Mouth of Truth).

Legend has it that people suspected of telling lies would be marched right up to the Bocca della Verità, located on what was originally the Foro Boario, ancient Rome's marketplace for cattle and livestock. Here suspects would be questioned, and as they answered, they would have to put a hand inside the mouth of this ancient stone relief. If the suspect told the truth, there was nothing to fear: The hand could be withdrawn triumphantly in one piece. But if the suspect decided to lie, the liar's hand would be chewed off, mangled, or withered within the grim unsmiling mouth of the Bocca della Verità.

HEY, KIDS!

Sorry, but researchers now believe that the Bocca was just a drain cover, probably excavated in the Middle Ages and moved here. Of course, the only way to test this would be to put your hand in the mouth, tell a lie, and see what happens...if you dare.

KEEP IN MIND The Bocca is a favorite with kids, although a half-hour visit is probably more than enough time, provided you miss the frequent busloads of tourists who stop here for a photo op. If it's too crowded, wait for a while on the lovely green grounds of two neighboring, recently restored second-century temples—the Tempio della Fortuna Virilis (Temple of Portunus) and the Tempio di Vesta (Temple of Hercules the Victorious)—located between the church and the river. They are surrounded by a patch of lawn that's perfect for an impromptu picnic.

Santa Maria in Cosmedin,
Piazza Bocca della Verità

 Free

 Daily 9–7

06/678.14.19

 3 and up

This is one of Rome's most famous photo opportunities as well as a great spot for kids to get the truth out of their brother or sister. Enter the porch of the church of Santa Maria in Cosmedin, just steps from the Tevere. To the left you will see a large flat round face with a small slit for a mouth. Have your camera and your probing questions ready.

Before you leave the church, take a peek inside, as few people who visit the Bocca della Verità ever do so. You'll find yourself in a serene 6th-century building originally constructed for congregations of Greeks, though it has been heavily restored. The church also provides some respite from the crowds and heat outside in summer.

EATS FOR KIDS Try nearby **Sora Lella** (Ponte Quattro Capi 16, tel. 06/686.16.01), on Isola Tiberina (Island in the Tiber). **Antico Caffé dell' Isola** (tel. 06/580.37.54), the connecting bar and gelateria, has nice sandwiches and great ice cream to take down the stairs and eat at the water's edge. Across the Isola Tiberina bridge in southern Trastevere, **L'Asinocotto** (Via dei Vascellari 48, tel.06/589.89.85) has excellent food, as does the **Taberna Piscinula** (Piazza in Piscinula 50, tel. 06/581.25.25). All these restaurants are within a 10-minute walk of the Bocca.

CAMPIDOGLIO

The lowest of Rome's seven hills, the Campidoglio (Capitoline Hill) is also its crowning jewel. Of any place you could bring your kids, this most easily connects them to both present-day Rome and its ancient and glorious past.

The Campidoglio is a traffic-free island rising above the chaos of Piazza Venezia, where five major thoroughfares career into one circle of screeching traffic. In fact, the only bad thing about visiting this fascinating site is that you have to risk your life to do it. Head for the zebra-striped lines, grab hands, and make eye contact with the speeding drivers. Assuming you make it across, you now have a choice: Take the steep pilgrim staircase, entering the Campidoglio through the Ara Coeli church (*see* Bambino Gesù), or take the *cordonata* (ramp) designed by Michelangelo for Charles V's arrival in Rome. Divide and conquer? Split up and meet at the top under the statue in the piazza's center. Time yourselves to see who gets there first and/or less winded. (Hint: Grown-ups, take the cordonata.)

KEEP IN MIND This piazza, its views, pigeon population, sculptural decorations, and constant pedestrian traffic provide a stress-free and stimulating overview of the city's history. Within just steps are numerous other sites you can combine with a stop here if the gang is game (*see* Altare della Patria, Foro Romano, and Carcere Mamertino). Need some bait to get your kids to take the museum's hook? Both the original of the statue of Marcus Aurelius and the world-famous bronze she-wolf, the symbol of Rome, are on display in there.

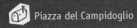

There's a hustle and bustle to this site. Many weddings occur daily (check listings under the loggia), government officials meet, and a glimpse of dignitaries or the mayor himself is common. All this activity takes place against a backdrop comprising stunning ancient statues of Castor and Pollux, colossal river gods reclining beneath an immense stairway, building facades by Michelangelo, and Rome's patron goddess, Minerva, dressed in her best red porphyry marble.

Just restored, the Museo Capitolino (Capitoline Museum) opens onto the piazza, from which the whole spectrum of Rome's past is seen. The uncontested best view of the Foro Romano spills out at your feet, and a connecting garden where Etruscans interpreted birds' flight patterns is now a serene spot to feed pigeons. To really join ancient and modern, note the equestrian statue of Marcus Aurelius in the piazza's center. He was the good emperor whose misguided son, Commodus, becomes the evil ruler in *Gladiator*.

HEY, KIDS! All the water in Rome's *fontanelle* (water fountains) is drinkable. Find the fontanella between the church and piazza, and cup your hand to block the spout. The cold, clear water will arc from the hole in the top, making drinking easier. Watch your timing, though, or you'll drench passersby.

EATS FOR KIDS Quick snacks (sandwiches, coffee, ice cream, fruit cups, and soft and mixed drinks) can be had at the **Museo Capitolino bar,** which you can access even if you don't visit the museum. It's worth the two-story climb as this spanking new bar has a huge terrace overlooking the city. Canvas umbrellas protect you from the heat of the day. For a full meal, cross Piazza Venezia to **Ristorante Abruzzi ai Santi Apostoli** (Via del Vaccaro 1, tel. 06/679.38.97), and order up the pasta *alla carbonara* (with bacon and eggs).

CAMPO DEI FIORI

This piazza is different from any other you will probably visit in Rome. What's missing? Unlike most piazze, this one has no church. And what's up with that statue of the guy in a hooded cape? He is Giordano Bruno, who, like many other heretics, was burned at the stake here during the Inquisition. When condemned to death in 1600, he told the judges, "You tremble more to give me that sentence than I tremble to accept it!" He went on to predict that the hallmark of any great society would be freedom of speech. Here in his shadow, you'll hear plenty of vendors exercising their freedom of speech in the morning open-air market. But that's only one reason the Campo dei Fiori (Field of Flowers) makes a great family destination. It's also the site of a cleaning "parade" at midday, soccer playing in the afternoon, and traffic-free outdoor dining in the evening.

In the very early hours, the piazza is quiet, but by 6, fruit, flower, and vegetable merchants arrive and set up their tables under the brooding statue of Bruno, as they have been

KEEP IN MIND Even if you don't have time or energy for a full tour of Via Giulia, walk the kids two blocks west to see the eerie facade of the church of Santa Maria dell'Orazione e Morte (*see* Via Giulia). It's a creepy reminder that death is indeed coming.

HEY, KIDS! What's a heretic? And what made Giordano Bruno one? He was considered a heretic (someone who asserts beliefs contrary to those of the church) because he believed that the earth wasn't the center of the universe, that there might be life on other planets, and that God, if he did exist, was mild and disinterested in humans. (The church taught that God was all-powerful and should be feared.) Bruno, like Galileo, was brought before the inquisitors to recant (take back) his beliefs. When he refused, he was burned at the stake where his statue now stands—erected 200 years later to honor freedom of speech.

Via dei Giubbonari and
Piazza della Cancelleria

 06/48.89.91Tourist
Information Point

 Free

Daily 24 hrs

All ages

doing since 1819. The campo then becomes a lively produce market. This is the perfect place to pick up the makings of a picnic.

The market runs until about 2, when the city cleaning machines arrive. The biggest trucks are called the *macchine madre* (mother trucks), and they are joined by a circus of sweeping and spraying machines that are fascinating for little kids. When the piazza is clean again, soccer becomes the international language; kids of all skill levels and ages can find kindred playmates here or ride bikes or trikes with the locals.

When homework responsibilities call, kids disappear and the campo becomes an open-air living room. Restaurants open, and the bohemian nightlife of this famous piazza begins.

EATS FOR KIDS Try the pizza *bianca* or the pizza *rosa* from **Antico Forno** (Piazza Campo dei Fiori 22, tel. 06/68.80.66.62), on the campo's north corner. For lunch, **Pollarola** (Piazza del Pollarola 26, tel. 06/68.80.16.54) is famous for its blistering hot cannelloni. It has a few outside tables. **Acchiapafantasmi** (Via dei Cappellari 66, tel. 06/687.34.62) has Rome's largest selection of pizzas, and **Montecarlo** (Vicolo Savelli 12, tel. 06/686.18.77) serves wonderful pizza at lunch or supper for astonishingly low prices.

CARCERE MAMERTINO

Ever wonder what it would have been like to be in prison in Roman times? Imagine being dropped into a cold dark underground room. Picture a neglected water cistern covered in mold, with only a narrow hole in its roof by which prisoners were forced to enter. This is what the Carcere Mamertino (Mamertine Prison) is like.

Nowadays, you can enter the dark and dank prison just under the church dedicated to San Giuseppe dei Falegnami (St. Joseph the Carpenter) without going through a hole in the roof. When you face the church, the entrance is to the right. Go through the turnstile, leave a small offering, and remember that for many pilgrims this is a sacred site. Silence, please.

The prison is on two floors, the upper dating from the second century BC and the lower from the fourth century BC. It consists of two small and miserable cells going back to Nero's reign. From the first room you enter, head to the left and down the narrow and irregular

KEEP IN MIND Even though you won't want to spend more than a half hour in this underground prison, you'll find the neighborhood alone well worth the trip. As you step out of the carcere, you find yourself on a set of stairs leading to various levels and landings overlooking the Foro Romano (see #48). If your kids don't have the energy to walk down into it, you can point out many of the highlights from wherever you pause.

Via del Tulliano and Via Clivo Argentario

 Donations requested

Daily 9–12 and 2:30–5

 06/679.29.02

4 and up

stone stairs to a small room, also carved out of stone. This is the lower cell, where St. Peter—with St. Paul, the patron saint of Rome—was imprisoned in AD 67. In the room's left-hand corner is a piece of the old marble column to which St. Peter was chained.

The miracle of St. Peter's stay here is told and retold by many of the pilgrims who come to see this site. It is said that he caused a spring of water to gush forth from the floor, with which he baptized his fellow prisoners and even the guards who kept watch over him. Here, too, in pre-Christian times, famous prisoners who resisted Roman rule were imprisoned, including Jugurtha, a king of Numidia, as well as several Gallic war chieftains.

Exit via the same steps you came down, but then turn left into a small book and souvenir shop before emerging into the light of day again.

HEY, KIDS! Why was Peter considered an enemy of Rome? Because of Peter's teaching and preaching, Christianity was becoming more popular, and people were unifying behind the idea that God was a higher authority than the government. So Peter was seen as a revolutionary and a threat.

EATS FOR KIDS It's a short walk to the old Jewish Ghetto and some of the best restaurants in Rome. Try **Il Portico** (Via del Portico d'Ottavia 16, tel. 06/687.47.22) or **Da Giggetto** (Via del Portico d'Ottavia 21, tel. 06/686.11.05). **Dolce Roma** (Via del Portico d'Ottavia 20B, tel. 06/689.21.96), the pastry shop nestled between these two restaurants, has great American and Austrian specialties, including chocolate-chip cookies, carrot cake, and Sachertorte, and both Stefano and Connie, the owners, speak English.

CASINA DELLE CIVETTE

59

Imagine a prince's house in a Roman garden that feels partly like a gingerbread house and partly like a Swiss chalet with a medieval twist. That's what the Casina delle Civette (Owl House) is all about. Built in 1840, the house was purchased by Prince Giovanni Torlonia in 1908, whereupon he redecorated it with medieval touches, living here until his death in 1939. Subsequently, the charming home was used as Anglo-American military headquarters, abandoned, vandalized, destroyed by fire, and finally—between 1992 and 1997—restored by the City of Rome. Today you can visit this fully restored and delightful residence and architectural curiosity, an homage to stained glass and Art Deco style.

Stunning and fanciful decorative details and jewel-like stained-glass windows fill every wall. Tour the ground floor first to see the exhibit of over 100 elegant watercolors and drawings done by master stained-glass artists and to get a sense of the house's layout. Both upstairs and downstairs present window after window of idyllic and whimsical flora and fauna in

EATS FOR KIDS The closest bar, **Tavola Calda Mauro Michele** (Via Zara 27–31, tel. 06/440.44.62) is a 10-minute stroll away. **Stella Maris** (Viale Regina Margherita 225, tel. 06/854.02.63) offers pizza at lunch, while **Eleanora d'Arborea** (Corso Trieste 23, tel. 06/44.25.09.43) is fancier. Or bring a picnic.

HEY, KIDS! Don't stop tracking down flora and fauna (plants and animals) once you get outside. When you exit the back door of this house, you'll find a bubbling little fountain and rock garden with a family of carved snails. In the vast adjoining gardens of the Villa Torlonia (where there are also swings and slides, rolling hills and umbrella pine trees) you may see real live animals. Check out the signs at the entrance to the park. They outline all the birds, other animals, and plants you might hope to spy.

Villa Torlonia, Via Nomentana 70

 €2.60 adults
18 and up

Apr–Sept, T–Su 9–7;
Oct–Mar, T–Su 9–5

06/44.25.00.72,
06/44.25.04.19 kids' lab

6 and up

what is called Liberty Style or Art Deco. Look out to the surrounding gardens through colored lenses, and go on an animal hunt. Is that chirping sound from real birds or from their stained-glass cousins? Search for the gorgeous wreaths, clover, and ribbons that are recurring themes. Careful observers can find luminous fruit, flowers, butterflies, bats, and swans as well as poetic scenes of swallows in flight, bulrushes, iris, grapevines, and arbors. Ivy details pop up in a chandelier, in *stucco* (plaster) work, and, of course, in glass. Look, too, for peacocks, yellow-eyed owls, and blue skies dotted with clouds.

A balcony of roses leads to a magical little round room decorated with ivy and ribbons. Don't miss the wooden passageway leading to a tower room and to a suite of rooms housing the Biblioteca delle Arti Applicate (Library of Applied Arts). This whole place is one big treasure hunt.

KEEP IN MIND It's the hunt for animals, plants, and brilliant colors that really turns kids on here. Suggest keeping a tally of all the different kinds of animals they find. If they're smitten by what they see, check out the *laboratorio per bambini* (kids' lab), where even children with limited Italian can participate in Saturday morning workshops for ages 8–12. Docents organize projects combining color, design, observation of the house's details, and imagination. Using transparent and black papers, children can make images with stained-glass inspiration.

CASTEL SANT'ANGELO

58

One of the city's most loved monuments and especially popular with kids, Castel Sant'Angelo combines a fortress, prison, castle, opera setting, torture chamber, mausoleum, temple, and museum. And though the cavernous multi-use space is fascinating in itself, it also sports spectacular views of Rome.

Built between AD 132 and 139, the monument was intended as a mausoleum for the emperor Hadrian, inspired by Augustus's tomb, north across the river. At the time, this spot was well outside town, so to connect it to the city, Hadrian built the Ponte Sant'Angelo (Bridge of Angels), later decorated with angels designed by Bernini.

Hadrian's original tomb was shaped like a big drum and covered in marble. On top, trees were planted, and all around the ridge were statues, of which the most important was of Hadrian on a chariot drawn by four stallions. This continued to be the burial place of many emperors for centuries after Hadrian's death.

KEEP IN MIND Linger in the lovely park that surrounds this monument. Shade trees and green lawn are dotted with benches, slides, swings, and seesaws, making it easy to spend the better part of a day here with children. Since cars aren't permitted on the grounds, many city kids learn to ride bikes or rollerblade here while nannies push baby carriages.

During the Middle Ages, popes fortified the original structure so that it could serve as a castle, prison, and fortress against invasion, and during the Renaissance, the mausoleum became known by its contemporary name, Castel Sant'Angelo. The bronze statue on top, depicting an angel resheathing his sword, commemorates a miraculous vision of Pope Gregory the Great. It's said that when he looked up and saw the angel of death putting his sword away, he realized a devastating plague was about to end.

To really explore all aspects of the monument, you'll have to go inside and outside; upstairs and downstairs; through narrow corridors, connecting rooms, and chambers; on a spiral ramp; and past piles of cannonballs, ammunition, and long-unused cannons. Several rooms are frescoed; others are bare. You'll see prison rooms, storerooms, an ornate library, and rooms that house a museum of weapons and armor. You'll see a lot.

EATS FOR KIDS

Castel Sant'Angelo's top-floor bar, **Bocchirin** (tel. 06/68.19.11.67), serves light meals against a backdrop of breathtaking landscape and architecture. The **Taverna da Giovanni** (Via del Banco di Santo Spirito 58, tel. 06/686.41.16, 06/686.15.12) is a short stroll away across the Ponte Sant'Angelo.

HEY, KIDS! When you look down on the bridge, remember that it wasn't always so lovely. It used to be lined with gallows. This is where many public executions took place, and bodies were often left to wag in the breeze as a reminder of the penalty for crimes. It wasn't until Bernini came along that the bridge got its Baroque facelift. Today you can walk past the angels, each of which is holding a symbol of the Passion of the Cross, including a crown of thorns, dice, and a robe.

CENTRALE MONTEMARTINI

57

Get ready for a *power*-ful experience at this unusual exhibition space, which answers the question "What does an old 1912 diesel electric power plant have to do with ancient art?" Here at Centrale Montemartini (Montemartini Center)—originally the aforementioned power plant and so also known by the electric company's acronym, ACEA—classical statuary is paired with early 20th-century generator equipment to make Rome's most innovative installation of antiquity in a modern setting.

Because of the space's expansive size—roughly 1,900 square meters (20,000 square feet)—children of all ages feel somewhat less restricted than in other museums in Rome. The collection includes over 400 examples of ancient sculpture, most of it from the vast holdings of the Museo Capitolino (Capitoline Museums). But what makes the museum so unusual is the juxtaposition of statues of gods and goddesses with machinery, levers, and wheels, both responsible for making and transmitting power in their respective times. In some areas, the machinery dominates, and massive turbines, tubes, and furnaces

EATS FOR KIDS **Voglia di Pasta** (Via Elvio Pertinace 1, tel. 06/59.60.45.43), closed Monday, specializes in *primi piatti* (first courses): pasta, soup, polenta. Get picnic fixings at the **Mercati Generali** (Via Ostiense). **Giappone** (Via Ostiense 110, tel. 06/574.41.90) has tempura and sushi.

HEY, KIDS! Have fun looking for examples of famous gods and goddesses. Can you find Apollo, who was both a Greek and Roman god? How do you know it's him? Try keeping track of how many times you see him and all the different gods and goddesses, with their distinctive attributes. Look for Achilles, Athena, Venus (Aphrodite), Jupiter, or Bacchus (Dionysus), and see if you can start to identify them without sneaking a look at the labels. Many of the Greek and Roman versions of these divine guys have identical myths and histories, and just the names change.

 Via Ostiense 106

 €4.15

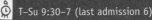 T–Su 9:30–7 (last admission 6)

06/574.80.30, 06/39.96.78.00 tkts

6 and up

dwarf the artwork. In other areas, colossal statuary vies for attention in front of engines and other equipment.

Until 2001, Sundays were Children's Day at this museum. All kids who entered received large sheets of paper, and all over the museum you could see kids happily sprawled and drawing. Activities began with the telling of selected ancient myths and legends in a story hour, followed in the afternoon by free guided tours of the collection geared especially to young children. The combination of the two brought the marble statuary to life for little ones. Unfortunately, these activities were discontinued for lack of funding, though there are plans to resume and amplify the children's education program in 2002. Call ahead to find out what, if anything, is going on. But even if no structured program exists, brush up on your myths and legends and enjoy this special museum with its spectacular collection.

KEEP IN MIND Rome's biggest market, the Mercati Generali, is just across the street. Restaurateurs and wholesalers flock here each morning to purchase the freshest goods possible in large quantities. You need to buy things by the case to get any respect, but even if you are not in a buying mood, it is a bustling scene not to be missed while you're in the neighborhood.

CERVETERI

Take a 45-minute drive outside Rome, and you and your budding Indiana Joneses can actually journey back in time some 2,500 years to this Etruscan town, home to a mysterious necropolis (city of the dead).

Actually, a good first stop is Cerveteri's museum, housed in a medieval castle in the center of town. Displays here tell much about the Etruscan people who populated this and other hill-town city-states before the Romans. Etruscans believed in an afterlife, so they had all sorts of items from daily life buried with them and carved into their tombs: tools and equipment, pottery, jewelry, cooking gear, carriages, votives, and even transport. The artifacts on view here were excavated from the local necropolis.

The big attraction for kids is not the museum, however, but rather the necropolis itself, about a mile from the center of town. Drive down the hill, following the signs. Here large dome-shaped tombs covered with grass dot a green park. Wander the gravel and dirt pathways

KEEP IN MIND Bring flashlights, as many of the more cavernous tombs are not well lit. Besides, having a flashlight in hand somehow raises the adventure level. Comfortable shoes are a must to maneuver the irregular staircases and dirt floors. Oftentimes some of the important tombs are closed due to heavy rain or lack of staff, so be sure to ask the guard what is open. For a tip, many guards will unlock such tombs as the Scudi e Sedie (Shields and Thrones) for you, even if they are closed.

from tomb to tomb. Maps of the tombs' layout, though not necessary, are available. Each tomb has at least one opening that leads down stairs to burial chambers. Some of the chambers are elaborately decorated, while others are rustically carved with simple shapes. Several have multiple entrances and multiple carved rooms, and most date from six centuries before Christ.

Check out the Tomba dei Rilievi (Tomb of the Carved Reliefs). Here, as in the other tombs, artisans carved the solid tufa stone and then painted the details, but the quality of the carving and painting sets it apart. *Sarcofagi* (coffins) were placed on shelves and spaces carved to resemble beds. In some tombs a glass barrier has been put in place to protect the paint from air.

So will young archaeologists find the lost ark? No, but they will find a maze of muddy floors, moss-covered walls, and eerie chambers to explore.

GETTING THERE Take the old Aurelia Antica north out of Rome. You'll soon find yourselves surrounded by pastures, orchards, vineyards, and fields and can catch periodic views of the ocean on your left. Then just follow the signs to Cerveteri, on the right.

EATS FOR KIDS In the center of town, **Cavallino Bianco** (Piazza Risorgiamento 7, tel. 06/994.36.93) is a good old-fashioned trattoria that's a favorite with locals. Have the homemade fettucine followed by any of the grilled meat selections. Otherwise, a picnic is the best bet. There are lots of great spots to spread out around the necropolis, which is bordered by farm fields. Pick up sandwich fixings at any of several small *alimentari* (grocery stores) in town.

CIMITERO ACATTOLICO

"It might make one in love with death, to be buried in so sweet a place," said Shelley. Of this cemetery, Henry James wrote, "...the most beautiful thing in Italy...it is tremendously, inexhaustibly touching, its effect never fails to overwhelm." Nestled at the base of Rome's only pyramid—that of Caius Cestius, built in 330 days in the first century BC—what's known as the Protestant cemetery is the resting place of artists and poets, visitors, and long-term Roman residents. Keats and Shelley are both buried here.

To enter, pull the chain by the gate to sound the bell. A gardener will let you in. The cemetery is divided into two parts. The older graves are through the wall on the left, with newer ones to the right and straight ahead. The oldest tomb, dated 1738, belongs to a British scholar named Langton, who died at age 25.

Visiting the Protestant cemetery teaches kids about the history of the Catholic church's intolerance for non-Catholics, buried here because they couldn't be buried on church property.

EATS FOR KIDS **Il Cantinone** (Via Bodoni 6, tel. 06/574.79.26) has a small outdoor sitting area and very good food at reasonable prices. For pizza, try **La Villetta** (Viale della Piramide Cestia 53, tel. 06/57.28.75.85). **Volpetti's** (Via Marmorata 47 B) carries Rome's most extravagant picnic fixings.

KEEP IN MIND This is still a working cemetery. You'll want to remind your kids to keep to the gravel pathways and be aware that some of the visitors are not here to sightsee but are friends and family members of the deceased and are coming to pay their respects. You may even encounter burial services, as the cemetery is still active. Still, you can make rubbings of inscriptions you especially like, sketch and draw freely, and feed the cats. Conveniently located benches allow you to catch shade or sunshine as desired.

 Via Caio Cestio 6

Free

06/574.19.00

Apr–Sept, T–Su 9–6; Oct–Mar, T–Su 9–5

8 and up

The church further insisted that non-Catholics hold their funerals at night and that tombstones not have crosses, refer to eternal life, or until 1870, even bear the inscription "God is love." If you keep this in mind, you can date many tombs at a glance.

Today the cemetery is one of Rome's most evocative and peaceful corners, though you may hear the hum of an occasional lawnmower. Fat cats doze in the sunshine. Towering cypress trees and boxwood hedges border the gravel pathways. The ivy-choked graves provide a moving and intimate history of non-Catholics, including foreigners, Jews, artists, writers, scholars, and philosophers who resided in Rome. Inscriptions are in English, Italian, German, Dutch, Swedish, and Greek, among others, and many graves are decorated with rose bushes and other ornamental plantings as well as potted plants.

A map of specific tombs and a guidebook in English are available for a small donation at the offices to the left of the entrance.

HEY, KIDS! Do some of the tombs look familiar? Perhaps one of the most famous and most moving of the 4,000 monuments in this cemetery is the *Angel of Grief*. A large winged stone angel flings himself over a tomb in desolation. Beneath, W. W. Story (writer and sculptor) and his wife are buried. A copy of this sculpture was erected at California's Stanford University in memory of the earthquake victims of 1906.

COLONNA DI TRAIANO

54

Like a three-dimensional spiraling book, the 19 huge drums of white marble that make up the Colonna di Traiano (Trajan's Column) serve as one of the world's most accurate and specific documents on war. In this case, the wars in question were those Emperor Trajan fought and won against the Dacians in AD 101–102 and again in 105–106. Battles and campaigns are carved into the monument in ascending order in a fascinating level of detail.

The height of the column—over 40 meters (130 feet) tall—was designed to equal the exact height of a hill that once stood on the site. It's not here today because Trajan had the hillside leveled to build the neighboring market complex, which you can also visit. The marble column sits on an enormous base decorated with shields and trophies and, though originally topped by a statue of Trajan himself, today is crowned by a statue of St. Peter. (The Christian replacement was made in 1587.) Notice the small openings in each drum; these are actually windows. Inside the column is a spiral staircase, which is no longer open to the public.

EATS FOR KIDS **Alle Carrette** (Vicolo delle Carrette 14, tel. 06/679.27.70) has great pizza. For Sicilian food, try the somewhat fancier **Melo** (Via Magnanapoli 6, tel. 06/679.63.66), closed Sundays. **Maharajah** (Via dei Serpenti 124, tel. 06/47.41.44) serves Indian cuisine in a fun, exotic setting, or see the Campidoglio.

 Via dei Fori Imperiale

 Free

06/69.92.43.07
Tourist Information Point

Daily 24 hrs

8 and up

To begin the story, look for the boats bridging the Danube River. From here on, the battles are recounted in pictures, with the figure of Victory writing on a shield marking the divide between battle tales. Originally, there was even greater detail recorded, but the minutia of each warrior, shield, horse, and banner was described with paint, which has since worn away. In addition to being a remarkable record of military history, this is also the mausoleum where Trajan's ashes were placed upon his death, though the early Christians removed them along with other interesting relics.

The carving beautifully documents the crowds and chaos of war, moments of diplomatic intervention, prayers for the gods' guidance, and the deaths and injuries of soldiers and horses. Because it's both a work of art and a puzzle, it's a history book your kids will probably be happy to read.

KEEP IN MIND If you can't make out all the details or forgot your binoculars, the Museo Nazionale della Civiltà Romana (see #36), in EUR, has casts from the original displayed at eye level for easier reading. If your kids' interest in Trajan is piqued here, continue on to the neighboring Foro di Traiano (Trajan's Forum) to see the mall-type complex he developed.

HEY, KIDS! Did you bring your binoculars? See if you can pick out the carvings of Emperor Trajan himself. Like a superhero in a comic book, he appears over 60 times in this scroll of events, usually on horseback and usually with his arm raised. You can find him standing on a wall addressing the Dacians or speaking to a group of female prisoners. Or look for him making sacrifices to the gods.

IL COLOSSEO

An old expression says, "While the Colosseum stands, Rome stands. When the Colosseum falls, Rome falls." You can see for yourself that the city's most famous monument, a hulking shell that once witnessed famous gladiator bloodbaths, definitely still stands.

Similar to many modern-day stadiums, this magnificent structure could hold 50,000 spectators (though its 66 entrances and exits could fill or empty its three tiers much faster than today's). Imagine yourself as one of them: Purchase your ticket, climb up the stone staircase, and gaze out from little bays over the arena and its hollow floor (the old wooden floor has been removed). Children may think it's just a cavernous shell, but with some information and imagination, you might be able to reconstruct the cheering and hissing.

You can see dressing room and cage areas below you and imagine the intricate passageways, ramps, pulleys, trapdoors, and lifts that would have moved gladiators and animals to the stage. You can still see some of the marble-lined seating areas, where huge awnings

KEEP IN MIND Lines can stretch halfway around the Colosseo on a busy day, but they're usually much shorter if you arrive in early morning or at lunch. You can also book tickets ahead. Excellent audio guides are available (inquire at entrance) to help re-create the Colosseo's dramatic history.

HEY, KIDS! Did you see *Gladiator*? The film's reconstruction of the arena was awesome and, according to most historians, pretty accurate, right down to the awning details and sand-covered floor (to soak up the blood). But the movie's story, like a lot of Colosseum legend, is full of myths and misunderstandings. For instance, one myth has it that the famous "thumbs up" and "thumbs down" gestures came from audiences deciding gladiators' fates. This, like the legend that Christian martyrs were thrown to lions here because of their faith, is not entirely true.

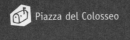
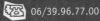

protected the audience from the sun. The best seats were at stage level, and it was here that the emperor and his family would sit along with other important members of society. The worst seats—for women and the standing-room-only crowd comprising the most humble classes—were furthest away. Interestingly, the gladiators themselves were originally prisoners or slaves, but over time members of the upper classes grew keen to fight as well. What started as a building project and diversion to counteract unemployment and the resulting dissatisfaction became a Roman pastime. People spent hours rehashing the battles fought here, discussing gladiator heroes and their remarkable feats.

The arena was inaugurated in AD 80 with games that left over 5,000 animals dead in 100 days. The last of the gladitorial battles was fought in 523, but nearly 1,500 years later people are still talking about what went on here.

EATS FOR KIDS Avoid the *bancarelle* (mobile food stands) surrounding the Colosseo, as they are quite expensive. Walk towards the church of San Giovanni in Laterano to reach **Binario 4** (Via San Giovanni in Laterano 32, tel. 06/700.55.61), for good local Roman cooking at modest prices. For a change of pace, **Baires** (Via Cavour 315, tel. 06/69.20.21.64) offers specialties from Argentina. Best of all, pack a picnic and head for the Monte Palatino (Palatine Hill), next door.

CRIPTA DEI CAPPUCCINI

"What you now are, we used to be; what we now are, you will be." This cheery greeting comes from the skeletons who inhabit the crypt of the Capuchin monks, or as it is more commonly called, the Bone Church, so named because exquisite patterns and decorations made of bone cover every surface. It's a macabre yet beautiful place, and looking around, you can't help but wonder how it came to be.

In 1631, an order of Franciscan monks—called the Capuchin because of the hooded brown habits they wear (*cappuccio* means hood in Italian)—was forced to move from the area in Rome where the Trevi fountain now is to their present location on Via Veneto. When they moved, they hauled the remains of their dead along with them and, rather than simply rebury them in their new digs, created elaborate environments out of the bones and body parts. The result is a stretch of corridor and six rooms, all decorated with bone.

Each room has a different name and theme based on the body part used. So you will find

KEEP IN MIND Unless human anatomy is your child's passion, a half hour is probably long enough to linger here. So why not visit the nearby Villa Borghese (*see* #6) and possibly the Galleria Borghese (*see* #46), too? And remember, this may be too creepy for sensitive kids.

the room of the skeletons (some dressed in brown hooded cloaks and holding crosses or scales) and the room of the skulls, with head after head lined up like cartons of leering eggs. Several rooms have inscriptions on the theme of death—"Death closes the doors of time and opens those of eternity," reads one—just in case you don't get the message from looking around you.

Little bone lamp holders and chandeliers sway above you. Archways and ceilings are decorated with bone parts. Backbone discs start to look like flowers, hip bones become the tile-like roof of a chapel, and jawbones form oval patterns and crowns. Here and there a tooth is left intact. An eerie commingling of body parts forms garlands of flowers and geometric patterns. But as horrific as the construction materials are, there is something oddly beautiful in these decorations, which gives you what the monks hoped for—a sense of triumph over death.

EATS FOR KIDS
The **Suggestum Caffé** (Via Veneto 14, tel. 06/481.97.08), across the street, serves light fare and fresh pastries. It has small tables to sit at if you don't want to stand at the bar. At the **Ristorante Pizzeria La Tavernetta** (Via Sistina 14, tel. 06/474.19.39), you can get a plate of pasta or more substantial fare, but it's closed Sunday.

HEY, KIDS! How many bodies does it take to yield this many bones? In the crypt's corridor and chambers you are looking at the remains of more than 4,000 monks and poor people who were recomposed as they decomposed. Scholars still don't know for sure where the inspiration for this bone art came from but suspect that limited space for burying the dead led to this creative solution.

EXPLORA

R ome's newest museum, subtitled Il Museo dei Bambini di Roma (Children's Museum of Rome), is also its only museum dedicated exclusively to kids. (No children can enter unless accompanied by an adult, and no adults can enter unless accompanied by kids.) Opened in 2001 in what was once a garage for public buses, the museum is just steps from Piazza del Popolo. Both indoor and outdoor space lets kids run around and explore structured exhibits, though some exhibits, especially those envisioned for older children, are still under construction. Still, younger kids find plenty to *esplora*.

The museum is organized in four sections. Extensive signage comes in English and Italian, and a large staff, many of whom speak some English, circulates to help the children. Io (Italian for "I"), the first exhibit as you enter, is designed to help kids get to know themselves and others better. A video on gestation and birth plays, and a doctor's office is re-created complete with an examination table, scales, and an X-ray viewer.

KEEP IN MIND When school is in session, the museum is often filled with school groups. It's wise to make reservations and come prepared for a high noise level. The modern architecture seems to make sounds reverberate.

HEY, KIDS! Don't miss the Identikit section, where you can make a face—literally—the way police artists do. Working from stacks of eyes, noses, and mouths, they reconstruct what criminals look like based on clues and witnesses' descriptions. Try making your own portraits of people you know by remembering what they look like and using the body parts provided. See how close your version comes to the real thing. If you'd rather take some artistic license, check out the area where you can create faces out of household objects, such as spoons, hair curlers, zippers, clothespins, and funnels.

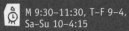

L'Ambiente (Environment) helps kids look at our homes, how we recycle, energy sources, and outdoor games. Clothes washers you can spin by hand, transparent toilets, refrigerators, and a full kitchen show how things work. Conservation issues are raised through measuring how much water we use to brush our teeth or flush a toilet.

Societa steers kids through a supermarket, mechanic's garage, fire-fighting equipment, water games, and artistic activities. By far the most popular spot here is the grocery store, where youngsters compete for the pivotal job of cashier. Last. Communicazione presents technology: a hands-on TV station where children can be the stars, computers, a bank (presenting the development of the euro), a post office, an underground city (showing wiring and gas pipes, etc.), and the telephone. Rome's only hands-on museum really does help kids learn firsthand about themselves and the world around them.

EATS FOR KIDS Picnic benches are provided, and you can pick up sandwiches at **Alimentari Bucchi** (Via Gianturco and Via degli Scialoja). **Bar 800** (Via Giambattista Vico 44, tel. 06/361.06.59), a favorite of nearby Temple Rome's faculty and students, has tables outside and excellent hot platters and sandwiches. **Ristorante Cesaretto** (Via Cesare Beccaria 3, tel. 06/361.08.01), open for lunch only, is perhaps one of the best lesser-known restaurants in Rome.

FONTANA DELLE TARTARUGHE

Four bronze boys, four marble shells, four leaping dolphins, and four small turtles make up the Fontana delle Tartarughe (Fountain of the Turtles), near the walls of the old Jewish Ghetto (*see* #45). Filling its piazza with the drumming of water, the fountain is a delightful place for kids to chill out while their folks people-watch, since its spray cools the air and everyone around it on a hot day. It's also a great place to slow down and sketch, and because its setting is so intimate and its scale so human, the fountain demands an intimacy of its viewers.

Walk around the fountain slowly. At first glance, each boy looks exactly like the other boys, but they are actually markedly different. Ask your kids which way the sculptor wanted you to believe the wind was blowing.

According to a neighborhood legend, a boy who lived in one of the houses here (Palazzo Mattei) was in love with a girl across the piazza. But he was a gambler, and her family

HEY, KIDS! Even though it makes a nice love story, there are other, more believable reasons besides heartbreak that people cemented their windows shut. Sometimes they did it to cut their taxes, since taxes were occasionally calculated based on the number of openings each building had on the main piazza. Sometimes windows were cemented shut simply because apartments were being renovated or redecorated.

Piazza Mattei

 Free

Daily 24 hrs

06/68.80.92.40
Tourist Information Point

All ages

didn't approve. To prove his worth, he had the fountain constructed overnight. When she awoke and opened her window, the girl couldn't believe how beautiful the fountain was and how the water drowned out all other noise in the piazza, so she fell madly in love and married him. Eventually she regretted her decision, moved back in with her parents, and boarded up her bedroom windows to shut out the sight and sound of the fountain. If you doubt this legend, look up at her bedroom windows, still cemented shut.

Whether or not you believe the story, you'll probably agree that this is one of Rome's more magical small fountains. It was built by Taddeo Landini, a Florentine sculptor, and set into the fountain base, designed by Giacomo della Porta. If the piazza and fountain look vaguely familiar, it could be that you saw them in the films *The Talented Mr. Ripley* and *Midnight on Earth*. But nothing compares to getting up close and feeling the spray.

KEEP IN MIND Fountains were Rome's way of celebrating the arrival of water as it was piped into neighborhoods. Before this one, the only other nearby fountain was in Piazza Cinque Scole, within the Ghetto walls. It was used by residents to wash themselves, their food, and their clothing.

EATS FOR KIDS On a little side street, **Zi' Fenizia Pizzeria e Paninoteca Kosher** (Via Santa Maria del Pianto 65, tel. 06/689.69.76) offers kosher pizza by the slice as well as other fast-food options. For the best pastries in the area, try the *fornaio* (bakery) with no discernable name or sign (Via del Portico d'Ottavia 2, tel. 06/687.86.37). The ricotta cheesecake with chocolate chips is famous, as is the Kranz bread, a sweet braided loaf with candied fruit.

FONTANA DI TREVI

You can hear it well before you see it. Try! When you are within a few blocks of the Fontana di Trevi (Trevi Fountain), stop talking and listen. Before you know it, you'll hear a thunderous roar coming toward you—a sure sign you're getting close to one of Rome's largest, most famous, and most beautifully riotous fountains.

The fountain was initiated by Pope Clement XII as the centerpiece of the intersection of three roadways. Completed in the mid-1700s, it was designed by Nicola Salvi, who combined many elements to create this full Rococo experience. As with anything Rococo, the fountain is asymmetrical, lighthearted, airy, and graceful. Salvi sculpted a scene that uses architecture as its backdrop, with ledges of rough stone and multiple figures in exaggerated poses. Tritons cavort and blow on seashells, and in the center, Neptune, god of the sea, is propelled by rearing sea horses. Huge chutes of water spurt from crevices—as important to the fountain's design as the sculptural elements.

HEY, KIDS!
The water in the fountain is known as Acqua Vergine (Virgin Water), because supposedly its source was shown to a Roman soldier by a young virgin in 19 BC. So if you believe the story, the spring has been flowing strong for over 2,000 years.

KEEP IN MIND The Fontana di Trevi is just a short walk from the Palazzo del Quirinale (Quirinal Palace), the official residence of Italy's president. Here at 4 each afternoon, you can watch the changing of the guard. If the president is in town, the show is especially dramatic because the *corazzieri* (president's guards) march in their fancy military uniforms along with the regular palace guards.

Piazza Trevi

 Free

 06/48.89.92.53
Rome Tourist Board

Daily 24 hrs

All ages

The Trevi is always jammed with crowds—and picture-takers—but always worth the visit. It is perhaps at its most beautiful when illuminated at night, so think about stopping by on your way to or from supper to see both the fountain and the surrounding nightlife. Kids of all ages find themselves shouting at each other over the water's roar and laughing as spray blows into someone's face. Like a huge stone confection dropped in the middle of the city, the fountain is so over the top that a carnival atmosphere prevails, even in outlying streets.

No one who wants to return to the Eternal City can help but stop here, since legend has it that to come back you must toss a coin in the waters. Stand with your back to the fountain and throw a coin (any value) over your shoulder. And no trying to fish coins out. Coins are collected weekly by the City of Rome for distribution to charities.

EATS FOR KIDS The streets are lined with very touristy pizza-by-the-slice places, but keep your eyes open for **San Crispino** (Via della Panetteria 54, tel. 06/679.39.24), one of Rome's best ice cream shops. Sparkling clean silver lids protect the ice cream beneath, all the ingredients are natural, and the result is delicious. For lunch there are two great choices: **Al Moro** (Vicolo delle Bollette 13, tel. 06/678.34.95) and the **Antica Locanda** (Via Lavatore 86, tel. 06/47.88.10.57).

FORO ROMANO

I f your kids are early risers, get them to the Foro Romano (Roman Forum) early. You may well have it to yourselves for an hour or so before the tour groups arrive. Alone you'll find it much easier to imagine how this dusty field dotted with marble ruins was once the center of daily life in ancient times.

Everything happened here: People met, deeds were signed, victories celebrated, goods sold, sacrifices offered, money exchanged. This was piazza, bank, market, temple, monument, and hangout. You might still sense the clamber and chaos of a typical day on these ancient roadways. As Stendhal wrote, ". . . imagine what is lacking and disregard what is there. . . ," but if you lack that imagination, pick up a guidebook before entering. Many have transparent overlays showing what monuments and buildings originally looked like, juxtaposed with a photo of the ruins as you see them now.

Free tours in English (inquire at the entrance) aid imaginations and interpretations. But

HEY, KIDS! Try to catch a glimpse of Mussolini's maps, just outside the Foro's main entrance on Via dei Fori Imperiali. Carved in marble, they show how the Roman empire expanded and shrank over time. One map shows Roman boundaries in the eighth century BC, while others represent 146 BC, AD 14, and AD 98, under the rule of Trajan. In the early 20th century, Mussolini himself wanted to conquer more lands and see Italy expand again as a world power. Do you suppose he envisioned his own map next in line? What might it have looked like?

if you go on your own, walk from one triumphal arch to the next—from the Arco di Settimio Severo (Arch of Septimius Severus, AD 203) to the Arco di Tito (Arch of Titus, AD 81), which documents Titus's triumph over Jerusalem. Both arches have exquisite carvings, telling stories of battles—the triumphant and defeated.

Stop at the round temple and house of the vestal virgins in the middle of the Foro. Here the eternal flame of Rome was kept burning, and important documents and signatures were kept. You can also take in the possible tomb of Romulus or the temple to the goddess protectress of the *cloaca* (sewer system)—that's right, a goddess to keep the drains unplugged! Good guidebooks map the highlights, but remember that too much information may make your kids' eyes glaze over. Take your cue from Italian families, who stroll here, sit on upturned bits of marble in the shade, take in the atmosphere, munch a snack, throw a few legends about, and then go and have lunch.

KEEP IN MIND The Palatino (Palatine Hill), too, is less crowded early. Enter from the Arco di Tito or Via San Gregorio, and wear sensible shoes, since the path is all uphill and dew can make things slippery. It's worth the climb, though, as it's decidedly cooler and kids can run more freely there.

EATS FOR KIDS Chances are your kids will tire long before you will, but you can extend your visit visually by dining on an expensive but delicious plate of pasta at the terrace restaurant of the **Hotel Forum** (Via Tor de'Conti 25, tel. 06/679.24.46). The views are unforgettable. Best of all would be a discreet picnic at the Foro or Palatino. Eating isn't allowed at either, but most guards don't enforce the rule. At the Palatino's Belvedere, panoramas spread at your feet and trees shelter you from the sun. Also see the Colosseo and Campidoglio.

FOSSE ARDEATINE

On March 24, 1944, Nazi SS troops took 335 Romans to abandoned caves on the outskirts of town and shot them. They then dynamited the caves' entrances and left the bodies to decay. The motive for this horrific massacre was retaliation: 10 victims for every German killed in the previous day's Via Rasella bombing, initiated by Romans in the Resistance, plus five extra victims. All had been prisoners of war in the Regina Coeli Prison, located on Via della Lungara in Trastevere. They included 73 Jews, a boy of only 14, foreigners, priests, professionals, and government officials, but none had had anything to do with the bombing.

Set amid greenery and flowering trees beneath the canopy of a cliff made of tufa stone, the site of this mass murder is now a stark and powerful reminder of the Resistance movement against the Germans. Row upon row of tombs contain the bodies of the victims found on site, and a huge slab of concrete marks their mass grave. A small museum dedicated to the Resistance is here as well and is a must for people interested in how the war scarred

HEY, KIDS!

During the massacre, peasants living nearby heard gunshots and later came here and witnessed what had gone on. They reported the massacre to the authorities, and through their efforts, the bodies were found.

KEEP IN MIND If a visit to this incredibly moving site has made your kids curious about the war, combine a visit here with a trip to the Museo della Liberazione di Roma (Via Tasso 145, tel. 06/700.38.66). This museum, documenting the war and Rome's liberation, is especially interesting for kids 10 and up. Geographically speaking, however, a visit to the Fosse Ardeatine is best combined with any of the sights on the Archeobus route (see #67).

 Via Ardeatina 174

 Free

 Apr–Sept, daily 8:30–6:15; Oct–Mar, daily 8:30–4

06/513.67.42

11 and up

Italy. But visiting the monument itself may be enough for your children. *The Martyrs,* a sculpture of huddled figures by Francesco Coccia, commemorates the terrifying last moments of those who lost their lives here. Mirko Basaldella designed a bronze gate and connecting wall of twisted thorny branches for this evocative site. Glittering and beautiful at a distance, the image of the piercing thorns becomes apparent only as you move closer. Every detail raises strong and moving questions about Italy's role in World War II, war in general, violence, politics, retaliation, and prejudice.

Take the time to walk through the further reaches of the park. The site's isolation becomes more apparent and allows you to feel more completely the profound power of this very moving and poignant memorial.

EATS FOR KIDS This is great picnic territory if you plan ahead. Wonderful food can also be had at **Hostaria dell'Archeologia** (*see* Via Appia Antica) or at **Ristorante Cecilia Metella** (Via Appia Antica 125, tel. 06/513.67.43), where the house specialty is served in little casserole dishes shaped like Metella's round tomb.

To get to this museum in the Villa Borghese (*see* #6), you need to walk through some of the park's rolling hills, passing joggers, dog walkers, and smooching lovers along the way. Eventually you end up at the huge 17th-century mansion where the Borghese collection is housed.

Visits are limited to two hours, which barely gives you time to let your eyes adjust to the glories and beauties of this magnificent mansion and its astounding collection of sculpture and paintings. For kids, the place can be daunting, so concentrate on the ground-floor collection—especially the six sculptures by Bernini, a great master of drama and movement who made stone seem simultaneously sharp and fluid. Check out *Apollo e Dafne*, which depicts Apollo chasing Daphne as she transforms into a tree. The bark begins on her stomach, and branches spring forth from her fingers and toes. Note the paper-thin carving of the marble. Bernini sculpted this when he was only 24! His sculptures reveal themselves most

HEY, KIDS! This mansion was built for the express purpose of exhibiting a specific collection of artwork. When you look at a statue, also look up at the frescoed ceiling. You'll probably find that the ceiling decoration corresponds to the piece of sculpture you are looking at. The frescoes are often other artists' interpretations of the same stories that the statues tell in stone.

Villa Borghese,
Piazzale Scipione Borghese

 06/328.10

 €6.20.
plus €1.05.
reservation fee

T–Sa 9–7, Su 9–1;
admission on odd hrs

 8 and up

fully if you walk all the way around them. As you circle each piece, you see how each one is a story with a beginning, a middle, and an end.

By contrast, the nearby *Paolina Borghese,* Canova's carving of Napoleon's sister as Venus, makes marble look as pliable as cream cheese. Buttery drapery melts over Venus's legs, and pillows sink beneath the weight of her arm. She stares out, seemingly detached from her surroundings if not from herself.

If your kids look well at these seven statues, that will probably be enough. If they have any energy left, however, they can head upstairs to find one more small Bernini sculpture. Called *Capra Amaltea,* the table-top statue depicts two boys and a goat. Though Bernini created it when he was a kid himself (under 17, according to documents), it already shows his masterful carving skills. Also take a gander upstairs at the Raphaels, Titians, and other great painting masterpieces, but be selective. It's easy to become overwhelmed.

EATS FOR KIDS
The museum's **snack bar** is quite good for a quick sandwich, pastry, or other snack, but the best bet is a picnic in the park. If you plan to explore the gardens, think about having lunch at the Galleria Nazionale d'Arte Moderna (*see* Villa Giulia).

KEEP IN MIND: You can only enter the museum for your two-hour visit at 9, 11, 1, 3, or 5, and reservations are mandatory. Plan on booking well in advance, and remember that you must pick up your tickets a half hour before your appointment. Though there is generally no line for tickets, there's usually a long line to check your bags—cameras, backpacks, and large pocketbooks are not allowed—so leave plenty of time.

IL GHETTO

Jews arrived in Rome before the birth of Christ. In 1555, however, Pope Paul IV, the great Inquisitor, confined them to a four-square block area that came to be known as il Ghetto. The area was surrounded by a stone wall, and inhabitants were locked inside each night from 10 in winter (11 in summer) to 8 the next morning. Denied most professions and the right to own property until 1870, Jews lived in poverty. Today the Ghetto is a lively and poignant reminder of the long and tumultuous history of the Jews here. Its streets are lined with fascinating ancient and medieval buildings, column bits, ruins, and spoils. Jewish merchants sell kosher foods, and restaurants specialize in fabulous Jewish Mediterranean cuisine. Sidewalks are full of elderly folk in folding chairs deep in conversation. The Ghetto is still about 60% Jewish, and most shops close on Saturday, the Sabbath.

Walking is the best way to see this evocative and vibrant neighborhood. Steer your kids down cobblestone alleyways and through the web of narrow streets. Visit the synagogue's Jewish museum, the Museo Ebraico di Roma (Lungotevere de' Cenci 15). Guides speak

HEY, KIDS!
From Portico d'Ottavia, look for the Teatro di Marcello, a rounded building with apartments and gardens. Completed in AD 13, it might be the world's oldest continually inhabited building. Many people hid from the Gestapo here. Now called Palazzo Orsini, it's one of Rome's exclusive addresses.

KEEP IN MIND
The more you know about Jewish history and World War II the more this neighborhood comes alive. Both the Jewish synagogue and the Menorah bookstore (Via del Tempio 2, tel. 06/687.92.97) provide excellent information on deciphering the significance of this area. Menorah has books on the Ghetto and Jewish culture and history in all languages. Families flood here to pick up souvenirs, postcards, Channukah candles, cookbooks, and scholarly texts. Still boggled? Book in advance with either Scala Reale (tel. 06/774.56.73) or Learned Travel (tel. 06/686.43.46), professional guiding services that offer insightful tours.

Piazza Cinque Scole to Portico
d'Ottavia and Lungotevere de' Cenci

 Free

Daily 24 hrs; museum T–F 9:30–2
and 3–5

 06/687.50.51 synagogue/museum,
06/48.89.91 Rome Tourist Board

 12 and up

fluent English and can thoroughly outline Jewish history here through World War II, when most of the neighborhood's inhabitants were deported to Nazi extermination camps. They'll also suggest local points of interest bearing testament to Roman Jewish culture and persecution. Sadly, the synagogue itself was the object of a drive-by shooting in 1982.

The Ghetto's main street, Via del Portico d'Ottavia, is lined with Renaissance buildings, and there are ongoing excavations at the Portico itself (149 BC.) The city's fine arts commission is housed in a freestanding medieval house (Via del Portico d'Ottavia 29), where a plaque recalls the neighborhood's World War II victims.

So for the ideal itinerary, wander Ghetto streets, visit its shops and synagogue, and enjoy a meal in one of its excellent and authentic restaurants.

EATS FOR KIDS For a full meal, try **Al Pompiere** (Via Santa Maria dei Calderari 38, tel. 06/686.83.77), especially cozy in the winter months. The best ice cream in the area is just outside the Ghetto at **Gelateria Alberto Pica** (Via della Seggiola 12, tel. 06/686.84.05), where the service is unfortunately surly. (They say all the family's sweetness went into the ice cream.) Or try **Pizzeria Franco & Cristina** (Via del Portico d'Ottavia 5, tel. 06/687.92.62) for pizza by the slice.

LUNA PARK

44

On the periphery of Rome, Luna Park, or Luna EUR as it's also known, is an old-fashioned European spin on the traditional American amusement park. Funky rides, eats, and games are set amid cypress trees, flowering hedges, potted pansies, an artificial lake, and stone walkways. Big fiberglass flowers spout water like fountains from Alice's Wonderland. Add to the scene pounding disco music; barkers calling out over microphones; strobe, neon, and flashing lights; and colorful banners snapping in the breeze, and there you have it: Luna Park.

"Something for everyone" has never been more true. Get your little ones directly to the outdoor puppet theater or the shining locomotive that circles the park and lake. Tots also have their choice of several carousels, a flying elephant ride, spinning teacups, long bumpy plastic slides, trampolines, and a ride called Splash Balls. Kids 7–11 find plenty of rides to choose from, including a rocking pirate ship, trampolines, bumper cars, and

KEEP IN MIND Once darkness falls, visitors are mostly older teens, so though it's great for people-watching and checking out the latest Italian teen fashions, daylight to dusk is best for families with younger kids. Luna Park is also bigger than it first looks and full of distractions. Circle the whole park before selecting rides, and then pick a meeting point just in case. Crowds make it hard to reconnect if you get separated. And if it rains? Although there are a few sheltered arcade games, most of the park depends on good weather to operate, so come when the sun is shining.

Via delle Tre Fontane

 06/592.59.33

 Rides €1–6, ½-day visits avg €15–25

 Sa–Su plus vacation and after-school hrs; call for schedule

 All ages

motorized rubber rafts you can take for a turn on the lake. Four classic (blood and gore) haunted houses dot the park's corners, but be warned: Legend and Horror House can be really scary for the squeamish.

Older kids should opt for Tacadà, a sort of huge roulette wheel that spins people around; Turkish Twist, which spins until you're glued to the wall; the roller coasters; a Ferris wheel; and rides called Flipper, Thriller, and Space Kickers. The Discovery Ride is not for the weak-hearted: you hang upside down and spin around, nearly grazing the ground.

Snack food stands, sandwich bars, coffee shops, and ice cream vendors are spread throughout the stroller-friendly park grounds, so snacking, riding, and snacking some more tends to become everyone's rhythm.

EATS FOR KIDS

American fast foods from hot dogs and hamburgers to cotton candy are all available, but don't miss the local fare: delicious sweet green olives you can munch on or sandwiches of mozzarella and tomato stuffed into nicely salted white pizza bread.

HEY, KIDS! Try to keep Disneyland and other new American-style mega-amusement parks out of your mind or you may be disappointed. The technology of the rides is far less sophisticated here, and the park is probably smaller than most theme parks you have visited. Thinking of old-fashioned carnivals and fairs will get you closer to the true flavor of Luna EUR.

MOSTRA PERMANENTE DI CARROZZE

If Cinderella's carriage hadn't turned back into a pumpkin, it might have ended up in the remarkable Mostra Permanente di Carroze (Permanent Exhibition of Carriages), just off the Ardeatina roadway. Housed in a modern 3,000-square-meter (32,000-square-foot) exhibition space, the museum is nearly all underground. Here you'll find not only vehicles collected worldwide—from Asia, Northern Europe, North America, Hungary (famous for coach making), Italy, and beyond—but also prints and engravings of vehicles and a wide assortment of saddles and bridles, harnesses and reins.

The carriages displayed reflect a wide range of uses, decorative styles, speeds, and comfort levels. Items more modest than Cinderella enjoyed include an American covered wagon and several wagons and carts used to transport goods. You'll see a chariot made for the movie *Ben-Hur,* a tourist jitney used in Rome through the 19th century, and a long sleigh from Denmark that looks like something the kids from Narnia would have used. Look for the first convertible top and the brougham, a sleek and lovely white vehicle with

KEEP IN MIND Though the museum is seldom crowded, school groups can boost the noise level considerably. It's worth either calling ahead to ask if groups are booked for the day you plan to visit or coming in the afternoon, after most field trips have left.

EATS FOR KIDS The closest restaurant, **La Dea di Roma** (Centro Commerciale Ardeatina 2000, tel. 06/51.96.28.01) is also a very good bar and *tavola calda* (a popular type of Italian eatery that doesn't have the full service of a restaurant). It offers both light fare and more substantial meals. If you came by car and are heading back towards EUR, try **O'Mastò** (Largo Carlo Salinari 13/16, tel. 06/541.34.48) for pizza and seafood.

headlights, made in Italy. Check out the examples of Victoria carriages, which were popular throughout the 19th century, and the somber Italian hearse.

Along with being visually delightful, one of the great things about a visit here is seeing how varied the world's modes of transportation are and have been. Adaptations to different climates, needs, terrain, traditions, cultures, and technology have yielded remarkable examples of people's ingenuity in getting themselves and their belongings from one place to another.

But perhaps the most wonderful thing about this museum is that kids can clamber and climb over many of the vehicles on display. They can sit on leather seats and tufted cushions and imagine the rocky roads their ancestors drove across in similar vehicles. Vivid imaginations will be able to create old-fashioned travel adventures: the trauma of changing wheels in muddy roadways, the romance of being carried by horses across town, and the thrill of sliding down an icy hill in a sleigh.

HEY, KIDS! By far the most beautiful fairy-princess carriage in the collection is the Berlinetta, a carriage made for Princess Sissi of Austria. The detail is breathtaking, with lovely dreamy landscapes decorating the panels under the side windows. It is gold with red trim and has spoke wheels and cookie-cutter-carved borders along its roof. What's more, its interior is as lush as its fancy exterior. Imagine it being pulled by two horses.

MUSEI E GALLERIE VATICANE

No trip to Rome is complete without visiting the Vatican's museums—even with the crowds and long lines. The best approach with kids is to concentrate on very few highlights, chosen in advance, but to be prepared to change your plans.

People of every age love the Galleria degli Arazzi e delle Carte Geografiche (Gallery of Tapestries and Maps), containing frescoes of Italy, its ports, and the surrounding seas. Look for maps with Rome or any other cities you have visited. This corridor is often overlooked by the stampede to the Cappella Sistina (Sistine Chapel), so stay to the sides of the traffic flow to enjoy the maps as you walk.

The Cortile Ottagon (Octagonal Courtyard) will be crowded, but it's one of Rome's most beautiful indoor-outdoor spaces, with astonishing statuary. Kids also like the Museo Storico (Historical Museum) with its papal carriages, coaches, chairs, armor, and uniforms, but call in advance to see if this wing of the museum is open, as it is often closed to the public.

KEEP IN MIND First, call ahead to make sure the Vatican is open; it closes for major saints' days and Italian holidays. Second, arrive at 8:30 or just before lunch to avoid the worst crowds (midmorning). Next, even if you've planned an itinerary, be flexible. Everyone else may share your priorities, so be prepared to visit lesser-known wings, such as the Museo Gregoriano Etrusco (Etruscan collection), Galleria dell'Arte Moderna e Religiosa (Gallery of Modern Religious Art), and Sale dei Vasi (Vase Rooms). Last, to get the most from your visit, bring binoculars to view the Cappella Sistina, and consider getting audio guides for older kids.

 Viale Vaticano

06/69.88.30.41;
www.vaticano.va

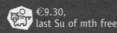 €9.30,
last Su of mth free

 M–F 8:45–4:45, Sa 8:45–1:45; last Su of mth 8:45–1; last admission 1 hr before closing

 10 and up

Still on the way to the Cappella Sistina, take time for the four remarkable rooms of papal apartments, decorated by Raphael. Background information in English is displayed. The intimate scale of the rooms combined with the hand of Raphael make them unforgettable, even to kids with limited patience for art.

In spite of the crowds, the highlight is of course Michelangelo's Cappella Sistina, painted 1508–1512 and recently restored to its mesmerizingly bright colors. Scene after scene of Bible stories unfold above you, and on the end wall, 20 years later, Michaelangelo painted the riveting *L'Ultimo Giudizio* (*Last Judgment*) fresco, a whirlpool vision of Christ condemning the evil to hell.

Since every square inch here is decorated with statuary, paintings, wardrobes, and shelves, let your kids' eyes feast on whatever interests them. The floor patterns alone could provide a lifetime of wonder.

EATS FOR KIDS

Avoid the Vatican cafeterias and head out to **La Grigliatta** (Via Germanico 170, tel. 06/321.13.12), closed Sundays, for classic central Italian cuisine. **Dal Toscano** (Via Germanico 58, tel. 06/39.72.57.17) has great Tuscan specialties, including hearty soups; quick, kind service; and an outdoor eating area.

HEY, KIDS! The *Last Judgment* took Michelangelo over seven years to paint, and he insisted on working alone. Notice that the figures on the left are being pulled up to heaven while those on the right are being forced into hell. Check out the ghoulish figure of Charon (lower right corner), who rows people to Hades in his boat and shoves them out upon arrival. Scholars say that the figure with the donkey ears in the middle of hell's flames is Biagio da Cesena, an acquaintance of Michelangelo's who dared to criticize his painting. To learn about fresco painting, see the Palazzo Massimo.

MUSEO CRIMINOLOGICO DI ROMA

C rime and punishment come to life (or is it death?) in this museum housed in the offices of one of Rome's most centrally located police precincts. Before you enter for your mandatory security check, look up at the 19th-century facade, with row upon row of barred windows. This is a former prison you are walking into, and the question ahead of you is, "Does crime pay?" You're about to find out.

The museum collection is divided into three sections. The first traces the history and development of the prison system in Italy. The second outlines the ways in which crimes are solved, criminals are caught, and motives are studied. No doubt your kids will enjoy both these sections, but they're likely to find the third exhibit, about the punishment of crimes, to be the most thrilling and chilling of all.

Here you see how crimes have been punished throughout the centuries in Europe. Instruments of torture are plentiful and include such famous devices as the Iron

EATS FOR KIDS Nearby are both the **Hostaria da Giulio** (Via della Barchetta 19, tel. 06/68.80.64.66) and the **Ristorante Monserrato** (Via di Monserrato 96, tel. 06/68.80.40.95), both with outside tables in good weather. Also see the listing for Via Giulia.

KEEP IN MIND Though children tend to focus on the instruments of punishment, what makes this museum unusual is its emphasis on how crimes are solved and how prisons work. Squeamish kids might like a psychological break from the torture devices, and that's where the ancillary exhibitions on how crime sites are reconstructed and how motives are studied come in handy. Braver kids should take the time to study some of the gruesome antique engravings documenting the instruments in use.

Via del Gonfalone 29

 06/68.30.02.34; www.polizia-
penitenziaria.it/struttura/museo1931.html

 €2.10 adults
18 and up

 M, W, and F–Sa 9–1; T and Th 9–1
and 2:30–6:30

6 and up

Maiden, a hinged spiked vessel into which offenders were placed. When the vessel was closed, the spikes tore into the perpetrator's (now victim's) body. Iron masks, instruments of suffocation, pistols, machine guns, and chairs with upright nails on their seats line the walls of this museum. A strange cage with a Sicilian skeleton hangs, casting bizarre shadows throughout the room. You'll see a guillotine designed specifically to cut off offenders' hands as well as nooses and an ax used by a notorious executioner. One of the guillotines was used as recently as 1870 and stands proudly on display next to a bucket to catch decapitated heads.

All kinds of crimes are outlined for your budding Sherlock Holmes, from art forgery to murder, robbery to terrorism, Mafia intrigues, and counterfeiting. You'll undoubtedly learn more about the Inquisition and its forms of torture than you knew before. Heretics, public burnings, hangings, and other executions are all carefully documented and will probably provide hours of fascination for strong-stomached kids.

HEY, KIDS! Did you know that witch hunts took place on a regular basis for hundreds of years throughout Europe? This museum shows some of the ways in which thousands of outspoken or nonconforming women were punished. And even though some of what is on display looks like ancient history, remember that many of these instruments of torture were used throughout the 19th century, only a little more than 100 years ago.

MUSEO DEGLI STRUMENTI MUSICALI

S hake, rattle, and roll. This museum of musical instruments has over 3,000 rare and unusual music-making devices. From oboes to music boxes, whistles to harpsichords, and phonographs to player pianos, this museum has a vast and beautiful collection.

Organized chronologically, the collection first displays very early archaeological finds. For instance, one room presents exotic ethnic instruments from Africa and Asia. Room XI contains instruments from the Middle Ages and early Renaissance, while Room XII holds instruments from the 16th and 17th centuries. Humble folk instruments mingle with instruments developed for church music or home entertainment.

Set in a large field next to the church of Santa Croce in Gerusalemme, the museum has some astonishing objects. Check out the painted 18th-century Neapolitan organ in Room XV. (If you are lucky, a docent will play for you.) It has an added eighth register made of 10 small lead pipes. When air is driven into a water-filled container, the pipes make a sound

KEEP IN MIND Though this is a "do not touch" museum, by calling ahead you may be able to book a guide who will animate some exhibits for you, including playing the piano. If the guide isn't available, ask one of the friendlier-looking guards to help. Just don't touch anything yourself! A visit here is nicely combined with the special-interest museum next door: the Museo Storico della Fanteria (see #32). But save some time for your children to enjoy the green park on Viale Carlo Felice. Here they can run around and play on swings within the shadow of Rome's old wall.

Piazza Santa Croce in Gerusalemme 9/A

 €2.10
18 and up

 T–Su 9–2

06/701.47.96

6 and up

like birdsong to accompany the music. There is also a beautiful Burmese harp from the 18th century that looks like a bejeweled sailing ship. Look for the music box with marionettes that move as a handle is turned; ask the guard to do this for you. You'll see the violinist bow his head as his arm moves, and a servant cools the performers with a big fan. Other displays include gorgeous carved harps, a tiny music box that teaches you bird songs, and chimes. An ivory bird caller is shaped like a delicate arc. Early pianos are beautifully painted wooden constructions, while the mandolins with inlaid mother-of-pearl detailing are breathtaking.

Only about 840 examples of the museum's vast collection are currently on display, but plans are underfoot to expand the exhibition space. Even so, seeing this portion of the collection is inspirational. You can't help but see how function, form, music, and performance all come together harmoniously.

EATS FOR KIDS
The closest restaurant, **Asia** (Via Santa Croce in Gerusalemme 1, tel. 06/702.21.58), is Chinese. You can get takeout for a picnic. The **Santa Croce Caffè** (Via Santa Croce in Gerusalemme 21, tel. 06/702.81.24) has very good, reasonably priced hot and cold plates, sandwiches, and pastries.

HEY, KIDS! Check out the small bronze statue of the *uomo-orchestra* (one-man band) in Room IV. It shows a 19th-century street musician poised as if to play the several instruments he carries—all at once. He's got a harmonica in his mouth, an accordion in his hands, a hat topped with tiers of bells, and a complete drum set tied to his back. Street musicians use fancy footwork. Each step they take pulls on a wire that clangs and bangs their drum set, and a toss of the head sets all those bells ringing.

MUSEO DELLE CERE

Abraham Lincoln, Hitler, and King Solomon. Rome's Museo delle Cere (Wax Museum) brings together the most unlikely grouping of characters imaginable. Put sophisticated waxworks like Madame Tussaud's out of your mind. This museum makes little attempt at realism. It relies on creaking floorboards, dusty dioramas, and the strange commingling of ill-proportioned wax figures to create an eerie and creepy atmosphere that is nevertheless not too scary for sensitive youngsters.

The exhibits begin with a 1943 meeting of fascist rulers sitting around a table, with Mussolini in the middle. The fact that all their heads are of differing scales and not in proportion to their bodies and that their hands are all the same adds a dimension of wackiness to the setting. These incongruities continue throughout the museum, but instead of being a distraction, they actually become what is most fun about the installations. What, for instance, is Dante doing talking with fellow poet Leopardi, since over three centuries separated them in real time? Should we care that they are conversing in what looks like a Victorian sitting room?

EATS FOR KIDS
Dunkin' Donuts (Via di San Vincenzo 1, tel. 06/69.92.48.38) is very close. For a complete meal, try the excellent **Al Piccolo Arancio** (Vicolo Scanderbeg 112, tel. 06/678.61.39). At **Sweet Sweet** (Via dei Lavatori 45), you can mix your own bag of candy.

KEEP IN MIND
Like many Roman museums, this one is accessed via narrow stairs. If you are maneuvering a stroller or wheelchair, access is particularly difficult. For a tip, you can leave a stroller with the *portiere* (doorman) on the ground floor. To make a trip to the neighborhood worthwhile, combine your visit to the wax museum with a foray to the Fontana di Trevi, Museo Nazionale della Pasta Alimentare, Palazzo Colonna (on Saturdays), or Time Elevator Roma (*see* listings for each), all of which are within just a couple of blocks of each other.

Piazza dei Santi Apostoli 67

 €4.15

 Daily 9–8

06/679.64.82;
www.museodellecere.it

5 and up

Sleeping Beauty looks like a man in drag. She breathes audibly, thanks to an old-fashioned air pump that makes her chest heave. Next to her are a couple of executioner's devices: an electric chair, a gas chair, and some gallows. Around the corner hover famous composers like Wagner, Verdi, and Strauss. Here you will see Italian heroes from the world of science (Galileo, Marconi, and Volta) as well as soccer heroes Nesta and Totti, representing their teams of Lazio and Roma. Wherever you turn, old tiles groan underfoot, and velvet flocked wallpaper and damask drapes greet you.

As funky and weird as the setting is and as awkward as the wax mannequins are, you'll still come away with a sense of Italy's popular cult figures. Do you know who Lucrezia Borgia was? Or Alessandro Volta? And what about the big display dedicated to I Pooh, an Italian rock group from the '60s? Who were these folks and what are they doing here? Come find out.

HEY, KIDS! No wax museum in Europe would be complete without a model of the Pope, but this rendering has a head that's way too big for his body, making him look more like one of the seven dwarfs. A good way to check proportions is to remember that the height of an average adult's body is about six or seven times the length of the head. Put your arm out straight, and measure the height of the Pope's head with your thumb. Then, keeping your arm straight, multiply that down the length of his body to see where the artist went wrong.

MUSEO DELLE MURA DI ROMA

A long, long time ago—between the 4th century BC and the 17th century AD—Rome built walls to surround the city and its outskirts and protect them from barbarians and other invaders. Originally measuring 19 kilometers (12 miles) long and 6–8 meters (20–26 feet) high, they averaged 3½ meters (11½ feet) thick. Today much of the concrete and brick walls still stand. If you were to walk the entire length, it would take you the better part of a day. If you don't have that kind of energy or time, a visit to the Museo delle Mura di Roma (Museum of the Walls of Rome), a small didactic museum, is an excellent alternative.

Enter the museum, and climb the narrow stairs. Here you can learn about the walls' history—including their route, planning, and restoration—through maps, documents, photographs, and illustrations. Exhibits range from original brickwork to drawings of the tools used to cut the stones for the monumental walls.

KEEP IN MIND Exhibits are documented with good signage in English, so kids who are old enough and patient enough to read the text will learn plenty of interesting stuff. Some of the language gets quite technical and detailed, though, so little kids may find it boring. In good weather, they can hang out on the *passeggiata sulle mura* (the stretch of wall open for walking) instead. Because of the scarcity of parking and taxis, consider taking the Archeobus (*see* #67) here and visiting other local sights, such as Via Appia Antica and its catacombs (*see* #8) and the Fosse Ardeatine memorial (*see* #47).

Porta San Sebastiano 18,
at Via Appia Antica

 €2.10

 T–Su 9–7

06/70.47.52.84

9 and up

You can even walk along a good long stretch—about 350 meters (1,150 feet)—of the original walls. In addition to getting a bird's-eye view of the huge walkway and walls, you get wonderful vistas of cypress trees and greenery along the Via Appia Antica receding to the distant hills of Rome. Along every 30 meters (100 feet) of wall was a square tower, 11 of which are still standing. The museum incorporates some of these towers as conference rooms. In addition, walls had several large doorways flanked by smaller doorways called *posterulae,* which served the limited needs of local traffic.

The biggest thrill—especially but not only for kids—might be the uncanny feeling that you're a defender of Rome yourself. Walk along the wall, scanning for possible invaders. Climb stone staircases and travel through narrow passageways. Through the narrow slits in the masonry, you can imagine being an archer, ready to take aim should the enemy appear.

EATS FOR KIDS

Reserve a garden table in the colombarium at **Hostaria Antica Roma** (Via Appia Antica 87, tel. 06/513.28.88). For lighter fare, there are snack bars several long blocks away near Piazza Epiro or slightly farther away at Piazza Zama. Or picnic along Via Appia Antica.

HEY, KIDS! Know what a *pomerium* is? It was a line that marked the perimeter of a settlement. In the case of Rome, it outlined a strip of land on either side of the city walls where you could not build anything, grow anything, bury the dead, worship, or carry any weapons. Check out the documentation on Rome's pomerium in the first exhibition room. You'll see traces of this line even today when you walk sections of wall.

MUSEO MARIO PRAZ

37

Rome is full of grand museums but, like most of Italy, has very few historic homes open to the public. This museum, however, *was* once a home, that of Mario Praz (1896–1982), the great *anglista,* an Italian who was a critic and writer on Anglo cultural matters.

His home was actually an apartment on the third floor of Palazzo Primoli. Praz moved here in 1969 with his collections, antiquities, and memorabilia. It appears that Praz suffered from a *horror vacui* (fear of empty spaces), as the apartment is packed floor to ceiling with art and artifacts. Walls are hung with paintings placed over paintings placed over paintings. Shelves are crammed with books. Objects and collections are displayed on every surface possible. Anyone who has ever decorated a dollhouse will be fascinated by the attention paid to minute details—every corner, hallway, angle, and nook. Collections of small wax figures, portraits—gathered from all corners of Europe and even Rome's flea market, the

EATS FOR KIDS **Ristorante Passetto dal 1860** (Via Zanardelli 14, tel. 06/68.80.36.96) is a lovely choice. You could also cross the Tevere and take in the eats and view at Castel Sant'Angelo (*see #58*) or walk to nearby Piazza Navona (*see #21*) for ice cream or snacks.

HEY, KIDS! The original bathroom has been converted into a mini-gallery that displays some of Praz's collection of 400 watercolors. The watercolors are all of interiors of homes, painted in such a detailed manner that they look as though they may have taken years to complete. In addition to just being interesting to look at, the pictures provide valuable proof of how people have lived in different time periods, right down to the patterns on their wallpaper and the throw pillows on their beds.

Via Zanardelli 1

 06/686.10.89

 €2.10

 T-Su 8:30–7:30

10 and up

Porta Portese—hand-painted ladies' fans, rugs, statuary, and furniture fill the spaces, united by themes and colors. For instance, swans reappear from room to room. Ornate furniture includes some rare examples, such as a portable writing desk (imagine taking that along on a trip instead of a laptop computer!) and a fireplace wood holder shaped like a huge kettle drum. What's more, the rooms are decorated exactly as Praz left them at the time of his death, right down to the tassels on the curtains and the spreads on the beds.

To visit this house is to visit the life of Mario Praz. In fact, in his writings on the philosophy of interior decorating he wrote, ". . . the setting becomes a museum of one's soul, an archive of one's experience." You'll learn a lot about his soul and experience here.

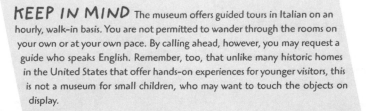

KEEP IN MIND The museum offers guided tours in Italian on an hourly, walk-in basis. You are not permitted to wander through the rooms on your own or at your own pace. By calling ahead, however, you may request a guide who speaks English. Remember, too, that unlike many historic homes in the United States that offer hands-on experiences for younger visitors, this is not a museum for small children, who may want to touch the objects on display.

MUSEO NAZIONALE DELLA CIVILTÀ ROMANA

Like many museums, this one is ideal for history buffs, but it's also ideal if you have stood confused and disoriented amid the ruins of imperial or ancient Rome. Having trouble picturing what old Rome actually looked like and how its people lived, raised their families, fought their battles, and farmed their land? This museum can provide the perfect point of reference and the key to understanding.

Anyone who longs to know how Roman monuments were constructed and how tools and early mechanisms actually worked shouldn't miss the rooms on construction, especially Rooms XXVIII–XXXII. Exhibits here explain the ins and outs of thermal baths: how the water was heated, transported (aqueducts), and stored (cisterns). The building and use of theaters, temples, amphitheaters, and basilicas are also documented. Other exhibits cover Roman family traditions, religion, portraits, law, music, and libraries, and the displays on medicine and pharmacies, agriculture, hunting, fishing, and commercial and financial life are fascinating. You may find Room XXXIII's information on road building and communication

KEEP IN MIND This museum occasionally offers educational, hands-on children's workshops based on daily life in ancient Rome, but they are often given only in Italian. Call for information. Guided tours are free and can be pre-booked (tel. 06/841.23.12) but are also offered only in Italian. But don't let a lack of language skills discourage you from visiting this educational and enlightening collection. Purchase the booklet in English at the entrance for general information on what you are seeing.

relevant as you wander today's Rome. And the plaster casts of important statues, reliefs, and inscriptions all help tweak your imagination and put things in perspective. Casts of Colonna di Traiano (see #54) friezes enable you to see the superb carving with much less difficulty than an on-site visit.

But the most stunning installations of all are the huge scale model of imperial Rome (with a scale of 1:250) and an equally compelling model of ancient Rome (1:1,000). These enormous and painstakingly constructed models pump you up to the size of God, remove all traffic and distractions, and reconstruct ancient buildings and neighborhoods in their entirety. By looking at both these models you are able to see how Rome evolved and expanded, as roads and population areas spread. The models depict important public buildings, roadways, surrounding agricultural lands, and the path of the Tevere. You can even trace the ring of aqueducts that provided Rome with its water.

EATS FOR KIDS
Columbus (Via Civiltà del Lavoro 96, tel. 06/592.61.50) has a restaurant, pizzeria, bar, ice cream parlor, and pastry shop, so everyone's cravings can be satisfied. Also see restaurant suggestions under the Museo Nazionale delle Arti e Tradizioni Popolari.

HEY, KIDS! It may sound like something from the *Flintstones*, but it's true: Ancient laws were carved into stones. You can see a cast of a Cippus stone from the Roman Forum, which outlines sacred laws in Latin. Be sure to check out the toys in the exhibit on family life in ancient Rome (Room XLII) and schools (Room XXXVI) to see how some things never change.

MUSEO NAZIONALE DELLA
PASTA ALIMENTARE

Macaroni, lasagna, penne, spaghetti, linguine, and more are the focus at this pasta museum. "Everything I am I owe to pasta," said Sophia Loren, who comes from Naples, where more pasta is eaten per capita than any other city in the world. But to find out about pasta and its history, you'll have to come to Rome.

Upon entering, ask for a CD player in English, and listen while you walk through the several small connecting rooms. Without the narrative, the museum wouldn't make much sense. You'll learn about the nutritional value of pasta. "If regular flour is silver, then semolina is gold," proclaims one poster. "And if semolina is gold, pasta is the joy of life," states another. You'll find out about the machinery that forms the varied pasta shapes (called draw benches) and witness machinery powered by hand, by horse, and by electricity. You'll learn about pasta's surprisingly simple ingredients and about its social history in different regions of Italy. Further, you'll discover that for just pennies a day, pasta could feed huge underfed populations worldwide and that dry pasta can be kept for years. Docents

EATS FOR KIDS With older kids interested in shopping and seeing the Scalinata di Spagna (Spanish Steps), consider eating at **Nino's** (Via Borgognona 11, tel. 06/678.67.52), en route. Also check out listings for the Fontana di Trevi, Palazzo Colonna, and Time Elevator Roma, all in this neighborhood.

HEY, KIDS! One of the more interesting displays here is the scale model in the glass case in the second room. It's a miniature replica of a factory for milling semolina to make flour. Note that the main source of energy isn't electricity, but rather horse power. You can see how the horses moved machinery that would in turn take the grain and grind it to produce the flour that was eventually used to make the pasta.

 Piazza Scanderbeg 117

 06/699.11.19

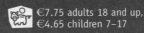 €7.75 adults 18 and up,
€4.65 children 7–17

🕐 Daily 9:30–5:30

🛒 8 and up

are happy to explain anything the CD player doesn't handle clearly enough.

Walls are lined with prints and photographs of people eating and making pasta. You'll see Sophia Loren with a huge plate of spaghetti as well as Paul Newman in a similar pose. Perhaps most amusing, however, are all the old prints of Neapolitans, heads tossed back, eating spaghetti with their bare hands in the streets. Here and there, advertisements for pasta brands through the ages document hundreds of shapes and sizes.

The museum is not without its oddities: Many paintings were commissioned with the caveat that they depict pasta shapes, resulting in some peculiar pasta-inspired art. And in a miniature theater exhibit on the lower level, a bunch of drinking glasses on a stage are filled with pasta shapes apparently imitating actors and actresses. It just may make you scream, "Basta pasta!" ("No more pasta!")

KEEP IN MIND An hour is more than enough time for this museum. The success of your visit will depend on your children's interest in the headphone narration describing each object. You can skip ahead over items that are less interesting. Ask at the front desk for directions on how to work the CD player to do so. Try scheduling your visit an hour or so before lunch so you can follow up your pasta research with a plate of the real thing.

MUSEO NAZIONALE DELLE ARTI
E TRADIZIONI POPOLARI

Located in the modern neighborhood of EUR, this two-story museum dedicated to the traditional arts, crafts, and secular and religious traditions of Italy is one of Rome's most popular museums for kids. What they (and you) will probably like here is that the exhibits focus on practical daily-life issues, including how things were made and done in the past and the cycles of life (birth, baptism, marriage, work, death) that have solidified Italian culture through the ages. What you may not like is that all the signage is in Italian. Just pick up one of the English guides (€2.60) available at the entrance.

The ground-floor vestibule is full of huge decorated carriages from Sicily. Upstairs there's a full-size 19th-century gondola that once carried Italy's queen, Regina Margherita of Savoy. In addition to modes of transportation, you'll find the world-famous Sicilian marionettes, mannequins depicting Italy's clowning traditions, and old toys, games, and musical instruments. Tools of various trades represent those used in wood- and iron-working, sewing and weaving, and cheese, olive oil, and bread making.

EATS FOR KIDS A **bar** at the museum offers the basics (ice cream, sandwiches, cold drinks); it's just across a small grassy area and under the loggia by the Museo Nazionale dell'Alto Medioevo. For more substantial fare, try the Corsetti Roma complex, which contains the **Vecchia America Birreria del West** (Piazzale Marconi 32, tel. 06/591.14.58), where hamburgers and other American favorites are highlighted. **Fiume delle Perle** (Via C. Colombo 312, tel. 06/511.03.76) is famous for Chinese food but serves pizza as well.

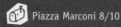 Piazza Marconi 8/10

 €4.15

 M–Sa 9–2, Su 9–1

06/591.07.09

8 and up

But the highlight for many families is the huge *presepio* (Christmas crèche) on the second floor. Here the nativity scene is set in a craggy mountainous landscape. Scores of lifelike figures play cards, eat supper, sell their wares, and make pizza and bread while baby Jesus and the holy family greet the three kings with their bounty of gifts. Presepi are a strong ongoing Italian tradition. If you happen to be in Rome over the holidays, you'll see scores of presepi in store windows, churches, and private homes.

Adding to the museum's richness, senior citizens volunteer as docents. Several speak a little bit of English and are anxious to explain family traditions of their own while pointing out objects of interest to you.

KEEP IN MIND
If the presepio was a hit with your kids, take them to the Museo Tipologico Nazionale del Presepio (Via Tor di Conti 31A, tel. 06/679.61.46). That's right. Rome has a museum devoted exclusively to nativity scenes; more than 3,000 crèches are exhibited year-round.

HEY, KIDS! The museum has more than 500 whistles in its collection, and many are on display. Some were used in religious celebrations, because it was thought that they had the power to banish evil spirits by making loud and varied noises. Some are made of clay (terra cotta), others of wood, and some look like highly decorated birds. Still others made a gargling noise when water was blown through them.

MUSEO SANITARIO

33

I s there a would-be doctor in the house? This medical-history museum is housed in a real working hospital, amid a maze of corridors, busy doctors and nurses, and rooms full of waiting patients. In fact, to get to the museum, you need to enter the Sala Alessandrina, a ground-floor lecture room decorated with medical prints and paintings depicting body parts. You may need to wait here until the custodian is available to escort you up the stairs to the collection. Note the marble top of a dissecting table leaning casually against the wall as you head up. It is a sign of things to come.

The Sala Capparoni houses early medical equipment and tools, sets of false teeth, and wax and clay models of organs. Everything is displayed in dusty turn-of-the-20th-century cases, making it feel as if you have chanced upon Dr. Frankenstein's inner sanctum. Check out the cases showing the veins and arteries of the circulatory system marked with thousands of little pins. It dates from 1844. Documents, an early wooden wheelchair,

EATS FOR KIDS Nearby **Sor'Eva** (Piazza della Rovere 108, tel. 06/687.57.97) is a small and simple eatery offering a full menu and pizza at very reasonable prices. A short walk due south, **Da Giovanni** (Via della Lungara 41A, tel. 06/686.15.14) is one of Rome's cheapest old-fashioned trattorias.

HEY, KIDS! At the end of the first large exhibition room are two adjoining rooms, replicating a 17th-century pharmacy and its laboratory. Check out the lab's authentic copper pots, pans, glass tubes, and vials full of healing powders, herbs, and pigments. Be sure to ask the custodian why that stuffed alligator is hanging from the ceiling—you'll be surprised at the answer.

 Santo Spirito Hospital,
Lungotevere in Sassia 3

 Free

 M, W, and F 10–12

06/68.35.23.53

10 and up

and models of the first metal wheelchairs line the walls. You'll also see a library of medical texts and a 17th-century birthing chair—a wood and leather oddity that makes you realize how far medicine has come.

The next room, the Sala Flaiani, is crammed with disturbing specimens of things that can go wrong in birth. Here fleshy embryos bob in liquid-filled jars on the floor, and skeletons with two heads grimace from ornate cabinets. Lodged next to dollhouse-like architectural models of hospitals, a skull labeled Pliny the Elder smiles. Cabinets hold compellingly beautiful wax organ models from the 1600s.

All of the objects here were collected and commissioned for the study and documentation of the evolution of medicine. The by-product of a visit can be fascination, horror, curiosity, repulsion, or all of the above.

KEEP IN MIND Some of the exhibits can be extremely upsetting if not viewed in the context of science and scientific study. The embryos and newborns bobbing in jars and the skeletons of actual babies with birth defects, such as two heads or enlarged skulls, can be terrifying to the squeamish. Consider booking a tour with the retired gynecologist here; his tours are given in a smattering of several languages and are best for teenagers on up.

MUSEO STORICO DELLA FANTERIA

To reach this museum on infantry history, wander through a large and untidy front yard littered with cannonballs, statuary, and a couple of old jeeps and tanks parked haphazardly next to somewhat unkempt shrubbery. Here a three-story Liberty-style (Art Deco) building houses not only exhibition space but also Rome's infantry school, and the grounds include a park. However, your first stop should be the office immediately on your right as you enter. Sign the ledger, and a young man in uniform will show you through the vast holdings of this odd but compelling museum documenting Italian military history. Few guides speak English and even fewer can give any concrete information on the displays, but much is self-explanatory.

Large models of battles occupy much of the space on each floor. For instance, the Battle of Zama (AD 202) shows Romans fighting in northern Africa. Warriors on elephants and foot soldiers hunkering down in ditches make this famous battle of Hannibal's come alive. Other models are equally detailed, including plumes of smoke and dismembered limbs.

KEEP IN MIND In spite of (or perhaps because of) its oddities, this museum is a favorite with older kids. If your troops become interested in the traces of war and the scars of battle, there are many other local sites that might interest them. Check out the nearby Museo della Liberazione di Roma (Via Tasso 145, tel. 06/700.38.66). Dedicated to the events of World War II, it provides an important link to the documentation you'll see here. Similarly, the Fosse Ardeatine (*see* #47), Rome's most moving war memorial, provides a valuable lesson on world conflicts and resolutions.

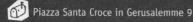

The museum also has fascinating models used to train soldiers. Check out the miniaturized war tools (Capproni airplanes, jeeps, and sandbags) as well as full-scale equipment (medical kits, saddles, and parachutes). Weapons such as bazookas, revolvers, rifles, swords, and knives are exhibited, and models of war environments, such as trenches, tunnels, mountains, and icebergs, show the development of military strategies and the adaptation of soldiers' gear. Compare the Alpine uniform complete with snowshoes and down mittens to the near-bikini dessert garb. Dusty display cases on all three floors hold over 100 uniforms, infinite varieties of helmets and other headgear, medals, weaponry, boots, and frayed banners.

Poignant acts of heroism are documented as well, as are the lives of Italian World War I and II commanders. Soldiers' diaries with drawings, poems, and unsent correspondence are painfully moving as is the colossal statue called *Il Partente* of a soldier father kissing his young son good-bye.

EATS FOR KIDS
Giovino e Nino's Ostaria Santa Croce (Via Santa Croce in Gerusalemme 33, tel. 06/700.94.65) is an Abruzzese restaurant specializing in good old-fashioned cooking at low prices. It has outdoor tables. See also Museo degli Strumenti Musicali.

HEY, KIDS! Camouflage is a pretty popular fashion statement nowadays, but its origins were about survival. Just like animals who manage to hide in nature, the patterns on clothing and equipment were developed to help soldiers hide in specific environments. A careful look at the uniforms displayed here reveals over 50 different fabric patterns and approaches to camouflage. Can you guess what type of place each was intended for?

MUSEO STORICO DELLE POSTE E DELLE TELECOMUNICAZIONI

From drum calls to smoke signals to Morse code and cell phones, this museum documents humanity's desire to make contact and communicate. Revolutionary technological inventions are presented here as are the Italians at the forefront of many of these radical developments. Some of the names will be familiar to you and your kids, and some will not—international heroes like Marconi and Volta and lesser-known (except within Italy) national heroes such as Meucci and Marci. Got a stamp collector in the family? In addition to covering world communications, the museum also honors postal systems and the hobby of stamp collecting.

This is one of Rome's great bargains (about 25¢ per kid), especially because the museum is so big. Over 20 exhibit rooms occupy a modern (1977) structure not unlike an earthbound spaceship, with circular staircases and long, snaking corridors. You travel roughly in chronological order, from ancient postal delivery services to a history of telecommunications, telegraphs, Morse code, telex, telephone, and the wireless. The last suite of exhibits

EATS FOR KIDS Viale Europa has many snack bars, fast food, and tavola calda places (between bars and restaurants on the eatery spectrum). **Ardito** (Piazza dei Navigatori 96, tel. 06/513.57.02) is a restaurant/pizzeria. **EUR-Cina** (Viale America 127–131, tel. 06/592.30.92), on EUR's artificial lake, offers a huge Asian menu.

KEEP IN MIND Because the museum is not open on weekends, your visit could very well collide with a large group of elementary and middle school kids, for whom this is a very popular field trip destination. Call ahead to inquire about a quiet morning to come, or schedule your trip for a week when Italian public schools are on vacation. Italian-speaking staffers are happy to share information with you, and signage is abundant (but also in Italian). An English-language leaflet available at the entrance (€2.60) should help to fill in the gaps.

 Viale Europa 190

 €.55 adults
18 and up, €.30
children 17 and under

 M–F 9–1

 06/54.22.16.73

 10 and up

deals with radio, television, and the Compressore Tosi, a pneumatic dispatch system that rarely fails to fascinate. (A similar but more extensive system is at Explora; *see* #51.)

Who really invented the telephone is one of the thornier issues this museum explores. It's a question still disputed by France, Germany, Italy, and the United States. Here the life of the Italian-born Meucci and his *telettrofono* invention—patented in 1871, some five years before Alexander Graham Bell submitted his patent request—are documented. The museum also presents a water telephone designed by Quirino Majorana and the first Italian 10-number switchboard created for the Vatican libraries in 1886.

Many people like coming here to see how things work—or, in the case of the Italian postal system, figuring out why they often don't. Considering today's fascination with chat rooms and e-mail, many others simply like gaining perspective on the historical importance of the spoken and written word.

HEY, KIDS! Keep your eyes open for Room 16, a fascinating reconstruction of the cabin of the yacht *Elettra*, where Marconi carried out his famous experiments for years. (Marconi is probably the most famous of the Italian inventors portrayed in this museum, and the *Elettra* was his floating laboratory.) The wood-paneled room contains original instruments used for radio telegraphy during World War II, which were rescued from the yacht before it sank in 1944.

ORTO BOTANICO

Chirping birds, gentlemen reading newspapers, and toddlers at play give this little pocket of green in a corner of Trastevere a serenity that seems almost too good to be true. Originally part of the vast land holdings of the Corsini family, the Orto Botanico (Botanical Gardens) were given to the biological vegetation department of Rome's university system in 1883. Divided into 19 sections, the park is a balance of highly manicured gardens and some less-cultivated, more-overgrown areas.

Start at the main entrance and ask for a map. There is no chance of getting lost, but the map highlights some interesting suggested itineraries. Follow the Viale delle Palme (Palm-lined Pathway) to the fountain of Tritons, surrounded by benches. In good weather, this is where the nannies, grandparents, and little children meet to play and snack, but at lunchtime, everyone disappears, heading for home and a hot meal.

Your choice of where to wander next depends somewhat on the season. If it's springtime,

KEEP IN MIND The beautiful Villa Farnesina (*see #3*), containing Raphael's *Galatea* and painted loggia, is just across the street. A good morning itinerary for a family could combine the art and architectural beauties of the villa with the freedom of wandering and exploring the botanical gardens. You're also not too far from the Museo Sanitario (*see #33*), just north on the Via della Lungara, should you have older kids in tow.

don't miss the fabulous collection of ornamental roses in the *roseto* (rose garden). Autumn is a great time to wander among the hardwood trees and collect their colorful fallen leaves. Rock gardens, a bamboo forest, a fern garden—most of whose plants are from Europe and central Asia—and greenhouses are terrific year-round destinations as well.

Don't get discouraged before climbing up the magnificent baroque staircase set into beds of lovely flowering plants. It will lead you to a Japanese garden with magnificent views. On your way back down the hill, stop at the little *lughetto* (lake), where goldfish and carp the size of steaks lazily paddle about. Close to the bathrooms and exit (pay phone, too), the lovely Giardino degli Aromi (Scent Garden) contains perfumed plants labeled in braille. Here you can touch and pull on the leaves to receive the perfume they offer, from lemon to geranium, oregano, and other herbs and spices.

HEY, KIDS! Of all the palm trees in Rome, there's only one that's native to Italy—and this park has several examples of it. To find it, go to the palm-lined path (to the left of the park's main pathway as you enter), and look for the *Chamaerops humilis*.

EATS FOR KIDS The **Caffé Settimiano** (Via P. Settimiana 1, tel. 06/581.04.68), on the southern corner of the Lungara, is the closest stop for sandwiches, pastries, and coffee. One of Rome's best *alimentari* (grocery stores) for the makings of a splendid picnic is **Pizzingrilli** (Via della Lungara 37/38). Try the nut bread with a sampling of the vast assortment of salami, ham, and cheeses. It is right next to the **Da Giovanni** trattoria (*see* Museo Sanitario).

OSTIA ANTICA

If the idea of visiting a buried city is calling to you but Pompeii is too far, take a shorter trip—just 45 minutes—to Rome's own buried city: Ostia Antica. Although nothing can rival the grandeur of Pompeii or Herculaneum, Ostia has a special seaside charm and a valid and compelling history of its own.

Ostia was founded in the fourth century BC and was a major port until trade began to diminish and the changing course of the river made the harbor less and less useful. These two factors coupled with outbreaks of malaria led to the city's abandonment and eventual burial in sand and silt. The site was excavated in stages through the last century.

In this great archeological zone, kids can run around freely and explore on their own. Point them in the direction of the Decumanus Maximus to find stunning black and white floor mosaics depicting sea creatures and other animals. The colored floor mosaics in the house

EATS FOR KIDS The expanse of excavations gives unlimited options for discreet picnicking. Family favorite **La Vecchia Pineta** (Piazza dell' Aquilone 4, tel. 06/56.47. 02.55, 06/56.47.02.82), right on the sea on the Lido di Ostia, feels like you're dining on the deck of an ocean liner.

HEY, KIDS! Ostia had its own version of Wall Street, Piazzale delle Corporazione, where big businesses from all over the world were represented. You can find traces of nearly 100 of its past occupants by looking at the mosaic patterns and decorations, made by fixing bits of marble into cement or plaster. From the mosaics you can determine the nature of each business and sometimes the country of origin.

Viale dei Romagnoli 717 €4.15

06/56.35.80.99; www.initaly.com/
regions/latium/ostia.htm

 Daily 9–1½ hrs before sunset

All ages

of the Dioscuri, with borders of dolphins and scenes of sea monsters, are just as fabulous.
There's an amphitheater (still used for performances in the summer), a Jewish synagogue, a
grain mill, bath complexes, and houses with courtyards to discover. There's even a bar with
a marble counter.

Don't miss the apartment houses, most of them four-story buildings and some still open
for you to climb up and see the view. Just as in Rome, most of them had shops or storefronts
on the ground floor and private living space above.

The layout of the city is instantly clear to even the most casual of visitors, and all the
major sites within the complex are labeled. Maps and guidebooks are available on-site
to steer your explorations.

KEEP IN MIND The temptation when you come to Ostia An-
tica is to combine your visit with a half day at the beach, Lido di Ostia. This is
not recommended in the summer months, as the water isn't clean enough for
swimming and the beachfront isn't kept as manicured it should be. On the
other hand, if you visit Ostia Antica in the fall or winter, a stroll on the lido is
a great conclusion to a morning of exploring the ruins.

PALAZZO ALTEMPS

One of the world's finest small museums, Palazzo Altemps provides a great museum outing with kids because the house is fun and interesting and because the collection is small but dramatic. Best of all, you will find no long waits, no crowds, and lots to see.

Two floors are open to the public. The ground floor encircles a beautiful courtyard with simple interconnected rooms full of ancient statuary—compelling for parents but perhaps monotonous for small kids. Upstairs, however, 20 lavishly frescoed rooms include the beautiful Sala delle Prospettive Dipinte (Room of Painted Perspectives). For a sure crowd-pleaser, step onto the fabulous loggia, full of intricately painted New World flora and fauna. Depicting a Garden of Earthly Delights, it's an ideal indoor-outdoor space for restless kids. While they gaze up, you can contemplate the portrait busts lining the loggia.

Don't miss the Studiolo della Clemenza, used as a study, and the Sala della Piattaia, a dining room with an unusual fresco of a china cabinet chock-full of wedding dishware. So many

HEY, KIDS! To glimpse the ancient Roman city on which this Renaissance palace (and much of Rome) is built, go to the ground-floor Sala della Torre (Tower Room). Here you can look at underground excavations that reveal bits of old Roman roads and buildings. Roman roads were built to last, as you can see. First a roadway was dug out, then came a sand and lime foundation, and then different-size stones measuring 1½ meters (5 feet) deep—the thickest part being the top layer of smooth paving stones—were laid. A slight swelling in the middle of roads helped rain run off.

 Via Sant'Appollinare 8

06/683.37.59

€5.20

T–Sa 9–7, Su 9–2

9 and up

of the rooms have such elegant friezes of fresco decoration that you must constantly remind yourself to look up and around to see all that the house has to offer. Set the kids on a mission to discover the whereabouts of the family chapel and sacristy.

Kids can compare two of the collection's highlights: In the Salone del Camino (Fireplace Sitting Room), *Il Galata Suicida,* a statue from Julius Caesar's private collection, depicts the horrible moment after a husband kills his wife and right before he commits suicide rather than live in submission to the enemy. Though it sounds gruesome, the riveting, stunning statue actually fascinates kids. By contrast, the Ludovesi throne, dating from the fifth century BC and the collection's most famous piece, shows Aphrodite's birth from the sea. In it she's lifted from the water by two maids, while the throne's side panels depict a flautist and priestess making an offering. Together, these treasures show kids birth and death in ancient times in a magnificent Renaissance setting.

KEEP IN MIND
Palazzo Altemps demands some concentration and good behavior from your troopers, which can be rewarded immediately afterward with a leisurely stop at Piazza Navona (*see* #21), just steps away. Make sure you peek at the underground ruins of the old stadium of Domitian.

EATS FOR KIDS Next door is **Passetto** (Via Zanardelli 14, tel. 06/68.80.36.96). It's a short walk to **Ristorante da Pancrazio** (Piazza Biscione 92, tel. 06/686.12.46), where you can dine underground in Pompey's ancient theater. Got a big appetite? Eat all you want from the fixed menu at **Ristorante del Pallaro** (Largo del Pallaro 15, tel. 06/68.80.14.88). For great ice cream, head to **Tre Scalini** (*see* Piazza Navona).

PALAZZO COLONNA

Every Saturday the Colonna family opens several rooms of their private home to the public. Now, most people come here to see the magnificent collection of more than 200 paintings and sculptures, including works by Rubens, Salviati, Botticelli, Bronzino, Tintoretto, and Reni, plus a throne room. But for kids, there are other more compelling reasons to hit Palazzo Colonna.

First, there are the ceilings, which depict wonderfully dramatic shipwrecks from the Battle of Lepanto. Ships collapse and slide into crashing waves. Drowning people struggle in the bowels of the sea. Great gory chaos reigns.

Second, for the shorter set, many tables lining the wall have gilt contorted figurines. Mermaids and prisoners grimace and writhe under heavy marble tabletops. Their dramatic poses are at perfect eye level for younger kids. And check out the huge ebony chest with ivory bas-reliefs. The white eyes of the black marble figures are especially eerie.

EATS FOR KIDS Next door, **Le Lanterne** (Via della Pilotta 21/a, tel. 06/69.92.44.58) offers an extensive menu with a wide selection of pizzas. Glass doors make you feel like you're eating outside even if you're inside. For other restaurants, see the Fontana di Trevi and Time Elevator Roma.

HEY, KIDS! The street you are on, the Via della Pilotta, was not named after a pilot, as you might think. *Pilotta*, or *pelota*, is the word for a leather-covered ball. Pilotta is also the name of a game that dates back to ancient times in Rome. Similar to today's handball, pilotta involved throwing a ball against a wall—in this case, the walls that lined and still line this street.

 Via della Pilotta 17

 06/678.43.50

 €5.20 adults 18 and up, €3.10 children 17 and under

 Sa 9–1

 10 and up

Third, notice the floors, which have great patterns and inlaid work. Some of the floors look like huge Rorschach tests with symmetrical marble vein patterns. Intricate oak leaves and acorns are cut into other floors in contrasting colors.

Fourth, check out the French clock that still chimes on the hour. At first it sounds like an alarm going off, a startling event in such proper quarters. Fifth, take in the cool views. You can see an oval interior garden from one window and a long cobblestone terrace from another.

But most important, in the middle of the Grand Salone stairs is a cannonball that smashed the marble steps as it flew into the room. According to one guide, the ball was misfired from the Gianicolo (go to Piazza Garibaldi at noon daily to hear the cannon) and crashed through a window. Another guide claimed it was fired by the French. However it got there, it's fun to figure out which direction it came from and which window it probably broke on its misguided trail.

KEEP IN MIND The beauty of a visit here is that the kids will have plenty to look at even if they never glance at any of the famous paintings that you yourself have come to see. But the recently restored Bronzino *Venere, Cupido, e Satiro* (*Venus, Cupid, and Satyr*) is one painting you will want to point out to them. Bringing binoculars so they can better see the ceiling frescoes of the Battle of Lepanto is also suggested, as is the well-illustrated and well-written guide to the galleries, available at the front desk.

PALAZZO MASSIMO ALLE TERME

Your kids' eyes may cross when they see the vast ground-floor rooms of exquisite marble statuary in this recently reopened museum (next to the train station), one of Rome's most splendid. Instead make a beeline for the top floor, and they should be delighted.

Upstairs, immediately to your left, enter a magical painted room from ancient Roman times—from Livia's villa, to be exact. This was Livia and Augustus's banquet room, then completely submerged beneath the earth to keep summer banquet guests cool. Even though there is not a window in the whole room, the garden scene is painted so that it seems to reveal a source of outer light. Frescoed walls show the artist's loving eye for detail. Nearly 70 different exotic birds are depicted perched or in flight, and nearly 30 different shrubs and trees line the garden walls. Look for oaks, pines, cypress, roses, daisies, blackbirds, swallows, and magpies. An incredible sense of luxury and lush abundance envelops you as you walk into these misty garden scenes. The painting seems timeless, as if the Impressionists had already begun working.

KEEP IN MIND If looking at paintings isn't grabbing your kids' attention, head for the basement of this museum to see the coin collection. Sound boring? It's not. You need to pass through the steel wall of a room–size safe to view these precious Roman coins, seals, medals, gems, and jewels. Best of all, to see the collection clearly, you get to manipulate elaborate magnifying glass machinery. Push the buttons and the metal arms and glass lenses move. Suddenly, detailed profiles swing into focus, and coins become living documents of past rulers.

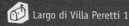 Largo di Villa Peretti 1

 €6.20

T–Sa 9–7, Su 9–1

06/52.07.26, 06/39.96.77.00 tkts

8 and up

According to historical sources, Augustus was so in love with Livia that he stole her from her husband, to whom she was quite happily married. Livia had a 3-year-old son and was pregnant with her first husband's child at the time. Even so, Augustus swept her away, and it seems Livia could not resist him. Theirs is the great love story of ancient Rome. Augustus apparently even turned a cold shoulder to Cleopatra's advances because of his marital happiness and fidelity. In fact, in spite of their scandalous beginnings as lovers, Augustus and Livia's marriage became a model for fellow Romans.

The rest of the upper floor is full of other examples of Roman painting and fresco decoration beautifully illuminated and displayed. Kids can walk in and out of vaulted chambers and one small painted nymphaeum (garden "room") after another, propelling them back to Roman times.

HEY, KIDS! To make these frescoes, powdered pigments were mixed with water and applied to fresh plaster. The two fused, and the painting actually merged with the wall, making it very durable in a dry climate like Italy's. Michelangelo used this same technique in the Sistine Chapel 1,500 years later.

EATS FOR KIDS You'll feel like you've been transported to the countryside at **La Gallina Bianca** (Via Rosmini 9, tel. 06/474.37.77). Choose from over 30 kinds of pizza, or try **Smeraldo** (Via Principe Amadeo 16/18, tel. 06/48.38.93). **I Leoni d'Abruzzo** (Via Vicenza 44, tel. 06/44.70.02.72), like the above restaurants, is close to the Termini train station, where, if little ones rule, you'll find a McDonald's.

IL PANTHEON

Of all of the monuments of the ancient world, including those of Egypt, Greece, and here in Rome, the Pantheon is in the most complete and original state. Located in a vibrant piazza in the center of a web of medieval streets, it was built on the site where the mythological founder of Rome, Palus Caprae, was carried off into space by the god Mars. In fact, the Pantheon means "of all gods," and it's one of Rome's most sacred sites.

The Pantheon is a feat of construction and building technology. The building is over 43 meters (142 feet) high and just as wide, and the walls are 7½ meters (25 feet) thick to support the dome. Walking into it from the sunshine, you enter a perfect transitional space, the porch, with shade provided by a grove of immense columns. Let your eyes adjust, and don't miss the enormous bronze doors at the entrance. From the Augustan period, they weigh about 18,000 kilos (20 tons) each and lead you into a great hall. Here the only

KEEP IN MIND This is a church, so church behavior is expected: No sitting or lying on the floor, though it's tempting. If kids start running, guards will intervene. If kids do need to blow off steam, head out front to the pigeon-filled but traffic-free piazza, or walk to Piazza Navona.

EATS FOR KIDS The area immediately around the Pantheon is full of bars, cafés, pizza-by-the-slice places, and sandwich shops. For more substantial fare, try **Fortunato al Pantheon** (Via del Pantheon 55, tel. 06/679.27.88, 06/679.36.83). Reserve a table outside. Other good choices are **L'Angoletto** (Piazza Rondanini 51, tel. 06/686.80.19, 06/686.12.03) or, just a short walk away, **Brek** (Largo di Torre Argentina 1, tel. 06/68.21.03.53), where you'll find a huge self-service menu, reasonable prices, and lots of indoor and outdoor terrace dining areas.

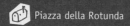

source of illumination in Roman times would have been the 9-meter-wide (30-foot-wide) oculus in the center of the poured concrete dome.

The Pantheon's history is likewise impressive—from 27 BC, when it was a pagan temple, to AD 608, when it became consecrated to the Virgin Mary, to the present, when it's used as a church and concert hall. The structure was the inspiration behind Michelangelo's design for the dome of San Pietro and for Brunelleschi's plans for the Duomo in Florence. Speaking of great Italian artists, look on the far left for the final resting place of Raphael, who requested that his tomb be placed in the building he loved most. Though it's the magnificent structure itself that you and your kids will most marvel at, chances are you'll be impressed by its over 2,000 years of history and influence, too.

HEY, KIDS! Check out the pitch of the floor. It is at its highest right under the oculus (the circular opening at the top of the dome) and slopes down to the edges of the building. It was built this way both to help drainage and to echo the shape of the dome above. You can best see the slant by crouching down under the oculus and looking at how people shrink near the walls. While crouching, also notice all the red marble on the floor. It's porphyry, the rarest marble in the world.

PARCO DEI MOSTRI

Giant monsters carved from stone, baby goats to feed, shade trees, and picnic benches. Just outside of Bomarzo, a sleepy little town about 1½ hours north of Rome, this is perhaps the strangest Renaissance garden in all of Italy. Known as the Monster Park of Bomarzo, the 16th-century garden, built by the Orsini family, is inhabited by make-believe stone creatures. The inspiration for the garden is still somewhat of a mystery, but mystery is part of what is so appealing about spending a day here.

Among the strange inhabitants lurking in these woods, you will find everything from an enormous stone turtle to a fighting dragon to a lumbering elephant. Eventually the winding dirt pathways find their way through the overgrown park to a huge monster's head with a gaping mouth—large enough for you to enter as a group. (There's even a banquet-size stone table inside it.) The monster leers at you from beneath the heavy branches of trees, and an inscription above it warns, "All thoughts flee!" You might want to as well, due to

HEY, KIDS! If you tire of wandering about the park, you may enjoy feeding the goats and sheep kept on the grounds. They'll come scurrying to greet you at the fence. Bring some lettuce or apples or cereal to feed them. If you decide to picnic here (benches provided), you may want to give the animals some of your leftovers. However, since they'll eat just about anything, *please* don't feed them things that aren't good for them, like junk food or food still in its wrapping.

Bomarzo

07/61.92.40.29 Viterbo Tourist
Information Agency

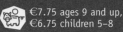 €7.75 ages 9 and up,
€6.75 children 5–8

 Daily 9–1 hr before sunset

 All ages

the Alice-in-Wonderland-gone-sinister feeling of this place. The carving is primitive, not elegant or refined, and the choice of subject matter (gargoyles, sphinxes, mer-creatures, wrestlers, and nymphs) leaves you with an eerie sensation.

Look for the little crooked house that you can climb up to have a partial view of the park around you. Even on a sunny day, the garden seems gloomy. The darkness of the stone combined with the thick greenery and dusty pathways is quite unlike anything you're likely to have seen before. And be sure to bring a camera to capture yourself and your loved ones inside the screaming monster mouth or waving from a window of the crooked house.

EATS FOR KIDS
At the on-premises **snack bar/self-service restaurant,** you can get snack food, pasta, or a three-course meal for under €10.35. For a change of atmosphere, head into Viterbo to **Porta Romana** (Via della Bontà 12, tel. 07/61.30.71.18), or see Terme dei Papi.

KEEP IN MIND The best way to see this area is by automobile. Although public transportation is available, it's difficult to meet its limited service schedule or get into the town or to restaurants without a car. While you're in the area, take a half day at the Terme dei Papi (*see* #12), enjoying the hot springs, or an afternoon in Viterbo, exploring the medieval section of the old city.

PARCO SCUOLA DEL TRAFFICO

T ired of having your kids be backseat drivers? The Parco Scuola del Traffico (Traffic School Park) puts kids in the driver's seat. Just think of it: Your kids can be taught to drive like the taxi drivers of Rome.

Located in EUR, the school is set in the corner of a huge rolling public park. Here kids get to drive not only minicars (ages 6 or older) but also the motor scooters the Italians call *motorini* (ages 12 or older), even if they can't ride a bicycle yet. The school has several *piste* (roadways) designed to teach about varied and safe driving environments. The roadways are dotted with small traffic lights, intersections, street signs, crosswalks, and rotaries, creating a real-world scene in miniature.

A fleet of 12 minicars in crayon colors is available. After signing up at the office and choosing their vehicle, children are taught how to accelerate, brake, and steer. Instructors walk or run alongside vehicles until it is clear that the driver is in control. Kids start off

EATS FOR KIDS The school sells snacks and soda but is a bit far from restaurants. Weather permitting, a picnic is the best bet. Or try one of Rome's few Mexican restaurants, the **Chattanooga Saloon** (Via Benedetto Croce 61/69, tel. 06/ 59.60.42.90), a modest drive away.

HEY, KIDS! All participants get a colorful workbook called "Guidiamo Sicuri" ("Let's Drive Safely"). It is well illustrated and easy to follow even if you don't read Italian fluently, especially because so many of the traffic signals are universal. In addition to reviewing street signs, you'll learn what to do in case of an accident; how weather conditions affect driving; how to park, pass, and change lanes; and basics of car repair and maintenance.

 Piazza Barcelona 10

 06/591.57.25

 One-time fee €3.40;
½-hr lesson, €7.50 car,
€8.55 motorino

Sa 3:30–6:30, Su 10–1 and 3:30–6:30

6 and up

driving on a big loop of roadway along the border of the park until they are skilled enough to enter the "highway."

This is a great destination in good weather and is ideal when combined with a picnic in the adjoining hills of the park. Paola is the gracious and well-organized director of the school. She supervises the excellent teaching staff, and her mother, a grandmotherly type, mans the traffic control tower, from which she calls out (albeit in Italian) such encouraging words as, "Go ahead, car 9. Proceed through intersection. You have a green light." Or, "Slow down, car 18. Tree ahead!" Despite the language barrier, most kids seem to get the gist.

Instruction is one-on-one, and the teachers are attentive and kind. Kids are given written material on traffic signals, safety, and rules of the road, and those who take several lessons and pass a test get a kid's driver's license from the Ministero dei Lavori Pubblici (Ministry of Public Works).

KEEP IN MIND The Parco Scuola del Traffico is outdoors and closes if it's raining. Besides, it's not very enjoyable in bad weather, since you might end up waiting in the car instead of watching. In case you were worried about a language barrier, don't. Instructors can give basic instruction in English. Since 1964 the school has been partially funded by the city government in an effort to make kids aware of traffic risks. As their booklet states, "Good drivers aren't born that way; they're taught that way."

PIAZZALE GARIBALDI

 it on a stone wall, and dangle your legs over the edge of the hill as Rome spreads out before you. That's what you'll find at Piazzale Garibaldi, where, from April to June 1849, volunteer troops led by Italian patriot Giuseppe Garibaldi fought invading French armies. (If your kids are old enough and have sturdy legs, hike up from Trastevere to get a sense of where this battle against the French was fought and eventually lost.) As you sit, see how many of Rome's monuments you can identify—from San Giovanni in Laterano's statue-bedecked backside (to your right) to the Pantheon (on your left), which looks like a big kitchen bowl drying upside down. The Palazzaccio, housing Rome's courts, glimmers white and alien, and wonderful green trees hug the whole length of the Tevere.

Try to time your arrival for shortly before noon and don't tell the kids why. They will be surprised by the explosion from a cannon that goes off with a terrifying BANG every day at 12. Even if you brace yourself, knowing it's coming, the report is enough to knock a filling out. The shot is heard all over Rome, and you'll often see people checking their watches

KEEP IN MIND Piazzale Garibaldi is close to Acqua Paola, one of Rome's splashiest fountains. Built in 1612, it boasts no figures, just arches, architecture, basins, and tons of cascading water. It's worth stopping here before or after your hike to the *piazzale* to cool off in the fountain's spray. The plummeting waters drown out any passing traffic sounds, and the view of the city across from the fountain is great.

 Passeggiata del Gianicolo

 Free

🕐 Daily 24 hrs

📠 06/48.89.92.53
Rome Tourist Board

🛒 All ages

against this daily reminder.

Small-scale puppet shows provide the occasional diversion. The hat is passed after episodes of Pucinello, Rome's famous clown figure—always dressed in white with a black mask—who constantly gets in fights. For more active toddlers, there are a carousel and old-fashioned pony rides around the piazza.

Statuary busts of famous Italians line the roadway, and a huge equestrian statue of Garibaldi himself rises from the pedestrian scene. The base of his statue bears the inscription ROME OR DEATH as well as a bas-relief of the she-wolf with Romulus and Remus, who, legend has it, were Rome's founders and first two kings. Around you, lovers snuggle, strollers stroll, the noise of Rome disappears, and the magnetically beautiful view remains.

HEY, KIDS! Look for the statue of Garibaldi's Brazilian wife, Anita, on a rearing horse with a gun in one hand and a baby on her lap. The statue, erected in 1932, marks her grave. To its north, a lighthouse that was a gift from Argentina in 1911 is illuminated at night.

EATS FOR KIDS The garden at **Scarpone** (Via San Pancrazio 15, tel. 06/581.40.94) is perfect for family lunches. You eat under an old leafy pergola, and kids have some room to run around. For a quicker bite, try the **Bar Gianicolo** at (Piazzale Aurelio 5, tel. 06/580.62.75), known as "Bar G," or, if you have a car, drive to **La Casina di Campagna** (Via Affogalasino 40, tel. 06/65.74.32.30), with pizza, etc., and a fabulous playground where kids can play while parents eat.

PIAZZA NAVONA

This oval piazza is Rome's most beautiful outdoor living room. Full of cafés and restaurants, the piazza takes its shape from the stadium of Domitian (check out the ruins at the piazza's north end), dating to about AD 86. Redecorated in Renaissance and Baroque times, the piazza is a jewel of traffic-free urban space. It's a great meeting point for kids, tricycles, strollers, and ice cream. At opposite ends of the piazza are two of Rome's most famous toy stores, loaded with everything from stuffed animals to Italian Lenci felt dolls, wooden Pinocchio toys, and kids' clothing. Of this piazza, the Italian poet G. G. Belli wrote, "It's a piazza, the countryside, a theater, a fair, a happiness," and it's all still true.

Dead center is a huge obelisk supported by Bernini's famous base, La Fontana dei Quattro Fiumi (Fountain of the Four Rivers), representing the Nile, Ganges, Danube, and de la Plata. Bernini's most successful fountain also depicts a massive grotto of travertine stone with huge river gods perched on ledges. Water is forced out of slots in the stone to form sheets that splash with tremendous force into the basin below. Unveiled in 1651, the fountain

EATS FOR KIDS **Tre Scalini** (Piazza Navona 30, tel. 06/687.91.48), the best-known of the piazza's eateries, is famous for its chocolate ice cream, known as *tartufo*. For less-expensive but great ice cream and huge servings, try the **Bottega di Gelato** (Via di Tormillina 15, tel. 06/686.56.57), a block off the piazza. For a full lunch, try **Da Ottavio** (Corso Rinasciamento 17, tel. 06/68.80.32.64) or walk to a Roman favorite, **Pollarola** (Piazza Pollarola 24, tel. 06/68.80.16.54) for their famous cannelloni. See also the nearby Palazzo Altemps.

Off Corso Rinasciamento

 Free

 Daily 24 hrs

 06/68.80.92.40
Tourist Information Point

 All ages

honors papal powers (note the river gods hoisting papal coats of arms) and celebrates water by creating a world of rock and water, splash and drama. While walking around it, look closely at the "place" Bernini creates: a world of carved animals, including a lion, horse, and sea serpents. A stone palm tree blows in the wind, and stone cacti grow from stone crevices. Seek out the armadillo and the sack of coins. Two smaller fountains punctuate the piazza's ends and add to the drum and hammer of water against stone.

Piazza Navona is also the city's most famous people-watching spot. People linger or stroll here to see or be seen. Kids with ice cream cones dash between the fountains, mimes, jugglers, and art vendors. Stone benches await those who prefer to sit and enjoy the show of architecture, fountains, people, and water.

HEY, KIDS! From December through January 6 each year, Piazza Navona is filled with Christmas *bancarelle* (stands). Games, shooting galleries, a carousel, and stands selling candy, ornaments, and all the makings for nativity scenes turn the piazza into Kids Central. It's a great time to visit, have your picture taken with Santa or the Befana (an Italian Christmas witch), and do some Christmas shopping.

PICCOLO MUSEO DEL PURGATORIO

This is without a doubt Rome's smallest museum, if not the smallest museum in all of Italy and perhaps the world. Housed in a narrow corridor of the sacristy of a neo-Gothic church, the entire collection fits in a glass display case about the size of a small coffin. But still, this museum poses an interesting question: Does purgatory really exist? The collection consists of about a dozen objects gathered by the Rev. Victor Jouet during his lifetime (he died in 1912), forming "proof" that it does indeed.

Purgatory, as documented by this collection, is located somewhere roughly half way between heaven and hell. People burn there until they have paid for their sins. How this is different from hell is something to ask the museum custodian.

To understand the significance of most of the objects here, take the time to read the one-page description on the table under the display case. Various stories are documented in several languages, including English, telling of ghosts who appeared to their loved ones, begging

HEY, KIDS! How does an odd museum like this get started? They say that Rev. Jouet got the idea for this museum when a fire broke out in his church. Where the altar stood, he saw a figure he assumed was a soul from purgatory. This became the impetus for him to collect information on other sightings of souls from purgatory and to convince the public that purgatory really does exist.

Chiesa Sacro Cuore del Suffragio,
Lungotevere Prati 12

 Free

 Daily 7:30–11:30 and 4:30–7:30

06/68.80.65.17

10 and up

for masses to be said on their behalf so that they could be released from purgatory. To prove their identities, these ghosts left burn marks that you can witness here. You'll see prayer books, sleeves, and chemises branded with fiery finger- and handprints.

Check out the nightcap of Jean Le Senechal, whose wife died in 1873. She came to him while he was sleeping to ask him to have masses said for her. In a moment of tenderness for him and to remind him—he was the forgetful type—she touched his nightcap and thus left the burnt imprint of her hand on it. This is perhaps one of the more convincing artifacts of the collection.

If skepticism is a family trait, you may want to remind each other to keep the wisecracks to a minimum until you're back out in the street. The museum is right in the sacristy of the church, and worshipers and church personnel pass frequently.

EATS FOR KIDS Hop over to Castel Sant' Angelo for a bite in its upstairs bar, **Bocchirin** (*see* #58), or try **Cesare** (Via Crescenzio 13, tel. 06/686.12.27) for a more substantial meal.

KEEP IN MIND Though the installation here is far from scintillating, kids do get engaged in what they are looking at if you read the stories provided on the handouts aloud. It also helps if your children are tall enough to peer into the display case (thus the older age group suggested above). Because the museum is so small, plan on about a ½-hour stay. Then follow it up with a visit to nearby Castel Sant'Angelo (*see* #58).

PORTA PORTESE

You enter Porta Portese, Rome's largest and most famous flea market, through a double-arched wall of the old city. Here, crowded against the wall itself and spilling into the street, are *bancarelle* (stands and stalls), barkers, and vendors from all over Italy. They set up at dawn, and by 9 or 10 the streets are packed with people-watchers, buyers, and sellers. Serious collectors shop early to get first pick of the new shipments.

The first impression you may get of the market is one of chaos, but older kids find it exhilarating. The air smells of peanuts, cotton candy, cigarette smoke, sausage sandwiches, furniture polish, soap suds, flowering plants, and the man standing next to you. You find everything and everyone at Porta Portese: antiques, new and used clothing, bicycles, plants, inflatable pools, folding chairs, kitchenware, shoes, toys, newborn puppies, bunnies, kittens, tropical fish, military memorabilia, bric-a-brac, ceramics, and furniture. Prices are lower than at most Roman shops, and bargaining is the name of the game. Ask prices, offer less, start to walk away, come back, and agree on a final price. Getting involved

KEEP IN MIND Crowds here are not for the fainthearted. Throngs pack the narrow roads, many smoking, others hoping to pick a pocket, so be careful. Strollers are very difficult to maneuver. Set a meeting place in case you get separated, or avoid the crowds altogether by coming very early.

HEY, KIDS! This is the cheapest place in town to pick up soccer shirts and scarves from your favorite Italian and other European teams. Try bargaining, and use sign language if your Italian isn't up to snuff. Even if you aren't in a shopping mood, check out the stands with old postcards of Rome, have an ice cream or sandwich, and go with the flow.

Enter anywhere from Porta Portese to Largo A. Toja

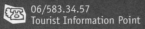 06/583.34.57 Tourist Information Point

 Free

Su 7–2

10 and up

in the theatrics of buying and selling is what Porta Portese is all about.

Most vendors are licensed, registered, and assigned fixed exhibition spots along the main corridors, to which they return weekly. Toward the edges, recent immigrants set up cloths on which they display objects from their home countries. You'll find Russians, Pakistani, Polish, Chinese, and other nationalities selling trinkets, spices, hand-crafted items, jewelry, and toys.

The open-air market actually winds its way through Trastevere from Porta Portese along the side streets south of Viale Trastevere for over 3 kilometers (2 miles). Like a street carnival with innumerable side shows, barkers, and heaps of junk and treasures, this is a Roman institution and not to be missed. It operates full throttle rain or shine (watch those umbrellas on crowded streets) and even on Christmas, should it fall on a Sunday. Just remember: Always offer less than the asking price!

EATS FOR KIDS Several street vendors sell *porchetta* (roast pork) sandwiches, sausages, or hot dogs. Others sell olives, candy, etc. Most of the bars and pastry shops flanking the market are open as well. For lunch, try **Papa Re** (Via della Lungaretta 149, tel. 06/581.20.69), **Il Ponentino** (Piazza del Drago 1, tel. 06/588.06.80), or the more elegant **Paris** (Piazza di San Calisto 7a, tel. 06/581.53.78).

SAN CLEMENTE

Did you ever wish time machines really existed? That in a moment you could go from one period of history to the next? The multilayered church of San Clemente allows you to do just that. Located not far from the Colosseo, this 12th-century basilica sits on top of a fourth-century church, which in turn sits on top of another layer of excavations, which have revealed first-century Roman buildings and a second-century Mithraic temple.

Start by visiting the church at its street-level entrance. Beautiful frescoes by Masolino depicting the life of St. Catherine decorate one chapel. Apse mosaics show garlands of greenery twisting around a central cross upon which white doves perch. A band of sheep completes the decoration.

To get to the underground portions of the church, go through the postcard shop, pay the small fee, and open the glass doors. You immediately feel the humidity from the vast excavations below. Walk down the broad steps past wall after wall embedded with bits of

KEEP IN MIND If it's a sunny day, get the underground chill out of your bones by sitting in the sun-drenched courtyard off the main church. It has a lovely fountain in the middle and is surrounded by a loggia with old granite columns. If your kids like this idea of underground Rome, they may also enjoy visiting the churches of Santa Cecilia (set upon a titular church and her family's original house and bath complex) and San Crisogono (built on an earlier church with remnants of frescoes still intact), both in Trastevere and both with vast underground excavation areas.

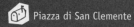

marble, ancient statuary, and inscriptions forming a kind of crazy quilt. Farther down you go. The more you descend, the earlier you go in time and the more narrow, twisting, dark and damp become the passageways. A greenish mold covers the walls, and what begins as the sound of dripping water grows to a roar of gushing water and sump pumps as you descend down, down, down.

To the left on the deepest level you can peek through bars to a mold-covered chamber with an altar in the middle. This was where bulls were sacrificed as part of the Mythraic tradition until the end of the fourth century. Further along this same corridor is a Mythraic schoolroom lined with niches and mysterious graffiti. Gateways lead to dark hallways. Vast rooms give way to tiny corridors.

In a visit of about an hour, the time machine of San Clemente will have permitted you to travel about a thousand years.

HEY, KIDS! The black-robed priests here speak perfect English but with an accent: an Irish brogue. They're Irish Dominican priests, and they have taken care of the church, excavations, and documentation since 1667. They're usually happy to share their wealth of information on the site and excavations, so ask away!

EATS FOR KIDS Even inside at **Li Rioni** (Via dei Santi Quattro 24, tel. 06/70.45.06.05) you feel like you're eating outside, but it's closed Tuesdays. This street also has a fun open-air **market** where you can pick up picnic foods. Around the corner at **Le Naumachie** (Via Celimontana 7, tel. 06/700.27.64), the pastas, grilled meats, and salads are terrific and at a good price.

SAN PIETRO

The mother church of all Christendom, La Basilica di San Pietro (St. Peter's Basilica) is visible from nearly every corner of the city. Bejeweled and bedecked in lavish decoration, the basilica welcomes thousands of pilgrims and visitors daily.

Be sure to approach from the Via della Concillazione so that Bernini's colonnade of 284 columns can reach out its arms to welcome you into the oval piazza, just as the artist envisioned. Take note of the fountains and the Egyptian obelisk in the middle before arriving at the portico and main entrance to the basilica. Once inside, give your eyes a chance to adjust, not only to the difference in light but also to the difference in scale. This is an immense treasure trove of art. To really appreciate it, pick up a guidebook (available at the bookstore on the left before you enter), which provides thorough information on each chapel, tomb, statue, and relic.

The whole family will recognize the church's most famous work of art, Michelangelo's

EATS FOR KIDS Avoid the food carts within the shadow of San Pietro, and head for **Matriciano** (Via dei Gracchi 55, tel. 06/321.23.27), with indoor and outdoor dining and classic Roman cooking. Its signature pasta has a hearty red sauce. Also see Musei e Gallerie Vaticani.

KEEP IN MIND Because this is such an important church, appropriate conduct and dress is required. Keep your shoulders covered, and don't wear shorts or miniskirts. To avoid the most congested times, come early or over lunch, when most tour groups are sitting down to a meal. If the kids are as good as all that San Pietro gold, reward them with a few secular hours at Extra Ball (Piazza Pio XI 31, tel. 06/39.37.70.74), a big family entertainment center with pinball, video games, shuffleboard, redemption games, and playground. It's open until 3 AM, in case your jet-lagged children are up late.

Pietà, located in the first chapel to the right as you enter. Even though you must now view it from a distance and through protective glass, the statue is powerful and compelling. Carved of marble when Michelangelo was only 25, the statue is the only one he signed (see the sash on the Virgin).

You can't miss Bernini's *baldacchino* (canopy) covering the high altar and his amazing *Cattedra di San Pietro* (Throne of St. Peter) just behind that. The four surrounding niches portray saints and their relics, including a statue of St. Longinus by Bernini. But from a kid's point of view, the real reason to come here is to climb through the dome, designed by Michelangelo when he was 81. (The entrance is by the Cappella Gregoriana; an elevator brings you partway up.) Be warned, though: Once you begin your ascent, you can't change your mind and come down. Parts of the climb can be a bit claustrophobic, as the stairway gets very narrow. Persevere, as the view is breathtaking from the top.

HEY, KIDS! How big is St. Peter's? Sometimes it's easy to lose your sense of scale in places this large. Walk down the middle of the nave and keep your eyes on the floor. You'll see bronze markers showing the length of other great churches around the world. Even Notre Dame in Paris could fit neatly inside this huge shell.

SANTA MARIA SOPRA MINERVA

E lephants in downtown Rome? Half the reason to bring kids to this church is the traffic-free piazza out front, containing the famous Bernini elephant (1667). The fanciful statue is ingeniously carved to support the weight of an obelisk. (Notice that the tassels of its saddle hide massive stonework.) Not surprisingly, it's a favorite of Romans of all ages.

Once your kids are hooked by the elephant, take them into the Dominican mother church (being prepared to hang out in the piazza if they get restless). Architecturally, the church has one of Rome's few Gothic interiors, but you can also see a sculpture by Michelangelo, two by Bernini, and first-class 15th-century wall paintings by Filippino Lippi here.

Start with the Lippi frescoes (1489) in the Cappella Carafa, the last chapel on the right. In addition to a beautiful airborne Madonna surrounded by angels playing musical instruments, you'll see scenes from the life of St. Thomas Aquinas. A tomb here belongs to the much-despised Pope Paul IV, who confined the Jews to the Ghetto in 1556.

KEEP IN MIND Before leaving the church, ask one of the priests if you can see the adjoining *cortile* (courtyard). Covered in decaying frescoes, it has remnants of an old temple to Minerva and leads to the rooms where Galileo was questioned during the Inquisition. You can combine your visit here with a trip to the Pantheon or the Stanze di Sant'Ignazio (*see* #25 and #13). A great view of both can be had from the roof terrace of the Hotel Minerva, to the right of the church entrance. Ask at the main desk for permission; they are usually happy to oblige.

 Piazza della Minerva

Free

Daily 7:30–7

06/68.80.92.40
Tourist Information Point

7 and up

A tomb under the main altar holds most of the body of St. Catherine of Siena. It's a major pilgrimage site, though some of her body parts are in Siena. To the left of the main altar is the sculpture of the *Cristo Risorto* (Resurrected Christ, 1514–1521), by Michelangelo. When it was made, it was one of his most loved sculptures. All along the side you can see the chisel marks where he carved. Check out his selective polishing as well as the masterfully carved arm and hand as they press against a wooden cross. It's amazing how close you can get to these works of art.

Both Bernini sculptures are to the left as you enter. Ask the priest to point them out. The carved bust is from a younger Bernini, whereas the Madonna on black marble was done later. If you find all these treasures, you will have seen the church well, and as a reward, there's an elephant waiting for you outside.

EATS FOR KIDS

For a splurge—and a great view—eat on the roof of the **Grand Hotel della Minerva** (Piazza della Minerva 69, tel. 06/69.52.01). Also see the Pantheon. For ice cream, try the **Cremeria Monteforte** (Via della Rotonda 22, tel. 06/686.77.20), to the right of the Pantheon.

HEY, KIDS! Do you know your Roman numerals? Check out the plaques on the front of the church before you go in (look up and to the right). How many of the dates can you calculate? Carved fingers point at waves, showing how high the Tiber's waters flooded in the neighborhood throughout history. The last time it flooded was 1870, after which the river's retaining walls were put in place.

SANTI COSMA E DAMIANO
MEDICI MARTIRI

It is Christmas all year around in the church of Santi Cosma e Damiano. When you enter the courtyard, turn to the right and enter a room where a fantastic Neapolitan *presepio* (nativity scene) is on permanent display. (Presepi are a longstanding Italian tradition thought to have begun in Naples, and many Italian families maintain the tradition of hand-making crèches in their homes.) The huge Christmas scene—16 by 9 meters (52½ by 29½ feet)—dates from the 18th century and depicts daily town life in amazing detail. Meals are eaten, wares are sold, animals carry heavy loads, and a flock of angels descends upon the nativity scene itself.

When you have had your fill of this visual feast, continue on to the main point of your visit: the basilica. This lovely church is graced with an astonishing sixth-century mosaic. Floating across a sun-streaked sky, Jesus holds a scroll in one hand and extends his other

EATS FOR KIDS If the weather is good, bring a picnic and munch discreetly in the Foro Romano or on the Palatino. **Alle Carrette** (*see* Colonna di Traiano) has a wide assortment of excellent pizza. Also see the Colosseo and Foro Romano.

HEY, KIDS! Early Christians had two choices about what to do with pagan architecture: tear it down or rededicate it to Christ. In this case, the pagan structures became the shell for this little church. This is most clearly seen when you first enter the building (look at the ancient wall on the right) and then again when you look out the back window of the church at the Foro Romano (just move the curtain aside). In both cases you can see the Roman masonry into which the church is set.

hand benevolently. He is dressed in his best gold outfit and is surrounded by Peter and Paul, who press forward to present the twin doctors Cosma and Damiano—Arabs who converted to Christianity—to him. They are dressed here in traditional purple doctors' robes with little medical pouches attached to their belts, as befits a church dedicated to these patron saints of all doctors. Check out the gory frescoes showing scenes of their martyrdom and miracles. You can pick out an angel putting out a fire intended to consume them and another scene with their beheaded bodies.

Peek out the heavy drapes in the back of the church, and you'll see a pane of glass that divides the church from its setting in the old Roman forum.

KEEP IN MIND If you are in Rome at Christmastime and want to start your own nativity scene, go to Piazza Navona (*see #21*). There stands are full of all the makings for Christmas scenes, including architecture, little fountains pumping real water, holy family figurines, palm trees, camels, and baskets of bounty. To see more presepi, check out the 3,000 on display at the Museo Tipologico Nazionale del Presepio (Via Tor di Conti 31A, tel. 06/ 679.61.46).

I s there any kid who doesn't like a day at the beach? Are there any adults who don't like picturesque seaside towns full of art and history? Sperlonga combines the best of both. Perched high on a cliff overlooking the sea, the village resembles a house of cards. Each house clings to its sun-drenched neighbor, while a white ribbon of sand waits below, accessed by long winding staircases from the town down to the water's edge.

From the beach, there is no better experience than standing knee deep in crystal-clear waters and looking back toward land. Above you is the whitewashed city covered in bougainvillea and vines, and to the right, like a magnet, is the dark mouth of the Grotta di Tiberio (Grotto of Tiberius). It was here that Emperor Tiberius entertained guests at a dining table surrounded by cooling waters. It's said that servants waded to the table and floated platters of food to the guests. Though you can no longer enter the grotto because of the danger of falling stalactites, you can have a good look at it from behind a protective barrier.

EATS FOR KIDS To avoid an extra trip up those daunting stairs to town, eat lunch on the beach. Pack a picnic of fresh mozzarella, and try everything the beach vendors offer. *Coco* is fresh coconut rinsed in cold water. *Grattacecchi* are cups of shaved ice drowned in flavored syrups. *Panini* are sandwiches available at the beachfront stabilimenti. For supper, try the pizzeria/restaurant **Tramonto** (Via Cristoforo Colombo 53, tel. 0771/54.95.97); the setting and sunset are as unforgettable as the food. The best crepes and ice cream are at **Da Filippo Fiorelli** (Via San Rocco 15, tel. 0771/54.11.62).

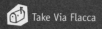 Take Via Flacca

 Free

Daily 24 hrs

0773/69.54.07
Tourist Information Point

All ages

Also on the beach, paddleboats are available for rent as are beach umbrellas and sun chairs. You can change in the dressing rooms of the *stabilimenti* (beach establishments) for a small fee or bring your own gear to the slim stretch of free beach.

Also take time to wander the old town—great for kids because cars aren't allowed in the center. Its walkways are staircases carved from the stone ledges of the city itself. Paths are covered with arches, and as you wander, you discover churches, terraces with beautiful views, beach-gear shops, and small groceries selling the town's famously delicious mozzarella.

A kilometer (.6 mile) south of town, you can tour the Museo Nazionale Archeologico (National Archaeological Museum, tel. 0771/54.80.28), built on the site of Tiberius's Roman-era villa. The museum holds beautiful marble statuary from the grotto and villa.

HEY, KIDS! Take the time to walk to the tower at the northern end of the beach. Locals say the original watchtower here on the water's edge defended the town from Saracen pirates, whose ships prowled the waters here centuries ago.

KEEP IN MIND If an hour-and-a-half drive seems too long, take the kids to the beach in Fregene, just a half hour from Rome. Check into Il Miraggio, a stabilimento where, in addition to the usual beach chair and umbrella rental, you'll find a wading pool and playground equipment that make a day at the beach memorable. Kids also love Aquapiper (Via Maremmana Inferiore, km 29,300, Guidonia Montecelio, tel. 0774/32.65.38), a water park also less than a half hour from central Rome. Kids up to 10 enter free if accompanied by an adult.

STANZE DI SANT'IGNAZIO

Have you ever looked in a carnival mirror only to find yourself all distorted and out of proportion? You're about to see a room frescoed to create the same effect.

It took 50 people over two years to restore the Stanze di Sant'Ignazio (Rooms of St. Ignatius). These rooms flanking the church of Il Gesù have been a pilgrimage destination for centuries. To see one of Rome's most wonderful and under-visited surprises, face the church, and look for the first door on the right. Enter quietly and talk in low voices. Follow the signs down the corridor to the right. Along the way you will see reproductions of prints about the life of Sant'Ignazio (Saint Ignatius of Loyola), founder of the Jesuits and builder of this church complex.

Go up the stairs on the right, and enter the first room, which was decorated in the 17th century by Andrea Pozzo, whose visual tricks and illusions continue to amaze us now.

KEEP IN MIND Pozzo's frescoes are next to holy rooms, where Sant' Ignazio lived and died and where pilgrims visit and Jesuit priests still live. Though hard, keep laughter and loud delight in control. If you're curious, go ahead and visit the adjoining rooms, but observe the *SILENZIO* (silence) signs.

HEY, KIDS! The room's center is marked by an inlaid marble rose. Walk backwards from it in any direction, and you'll see everything tilt and swell out of proportion. Choose one thing—say, a cherub—and keep your eyes on it no matter where you walk. Look at the size of the cherub's legs as you move. Count the steps back to the rose until everything is back in focus. How did the artist do this? Pozzo wrote a whole book on perspective, explaining how math and proportion affect visual arts. But even without understanding it, you'll think his work is pretty awesome.

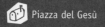 Piazza del Gesù

 06/68.80.92.40
Tourist Information Point

Free

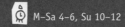 M–Sa 4–6, Su 10–12

8 and up

This is sophisticated and playful wall painting at its best. Pozzo's fascination with perspective created what seems like a cross between Escher and the Cappella Sistina, a three-dimensional board game designed for you to view while standing in the middle. But can you find the middle? Give up? Read the Hey, Kids! box below.

From the center, all seems right with the world. Little cherubs lift armfuls of flowers. Beams support complex and ornate architecture. Inscriptions are legible. Now move. From each end of the corridor, distortion and chaos reign. As you shift, the whole room morphs. Beams bend like spaghetti, and what seemed to be a chapel at the far end is just a flat wall. Walk backward to the center again, and watch the decoration slip back into its correct proportions, as order is again restored.

EATS FOR KIDS The closest and most fun of the nearby places to eat, the **Silent Music Café** (Via Celsa 7/b, tel. 06/679.35.66), is right off Piazza del Gesù. Munch on bruschetta and create your own salad. **La Carbonara** (Piazza Campo dei Fiori 23, tel. 06/686.47.83) isn't far either, and you can eat outside there. For ice cream, head toward the Pantheon and **Della Palma** (Via della Maddalena 20/23, tel. 06/68.80.67.52).

TERME DEI PAPI

On a clear day you can see plumes of steam from miles away. The steam is rising from the pool of this modern hot spring complex, named for its original use as papal baths. Fed by the Bullicame hot spring, the Terme dei Papi offers a delightful year-round break from Rome's often hectic pace. Once immersed in these splendid waters, you float effortlessly because the water's high content of calcium, sulphur, and other minerals makes you more buoyant. In addition to letting you float (or swim), however, these waters can supposedly cure you of whatever ails you.

Curative hot-spring baths have been popular in Italy since ancient times. Today the Terme dei Papi provide the largest full-service hot pools and related cures near Rome. A 15-page brochure (also available on the Web site) outlines the extensive massages, mud baths, and health treatments this hotel/hot spring complex offers. But even if you're not ailing, the trip is a delight.

KEEP IN MIND Bring a small padlock with you (or purchase one at the desk) to secure your valuables in a locker. You'll also want to bring a robe, flip-flops, bathing cap, and towel. Dressing rooms are equipped with hair dryers. If this European spa doesn't please the troops, you can try one of Rome's modern U.S.-style water parks. Idromania Acquapark (Vicolo Casale Lumbroso 200, tel. 06/618.31.83) has extensive slides, tidal pools, water works, and games that are sure to cool down your overheated kids. Also see the listing for Sperlonga for a well-deserved day at the beach.

 Strada Bagni 12, Viterbo

07/61.35.01;
www.termedeipapi.it

 Ages 13 and up €10.35
M–F, €12.95
Sa–Su; €5.20
children 1–12

 Daily 9–6; varies some with season

All ages

Swim laps or wade as your energy dictates. Can't stand the heat? Lots of people find the water source too hot to take. Just move away from the spouts of steaming water to the areas where cold water is pumped in. If you want to dry-dock for a while, rent a lounge chair. Older teens might enjoy the splurge of a facial or mud treatment while Mom and Dad relax in the sauna or indulge in a massage. There is even a steam bath set within a grotto.

On weekends and holidays, the baths offer a Mini-Club. For €20.70, kids can have a full day (10–4) of organized programs, including admission, supervision, lunch, a snack, and activities and games both in and out of the water.

To make getting here easier, a shuttle bus leaves Piazza Mancini at 8:30, arriving at the baths at 9:45. A return bus leaves at 1:15, arriving at 2:30. Reservations, which are necessary, can be made by calling the number above.

HEY, KIDS! That smell of rotten eggs comes from the water's high sulfur content. It may even linger in your towels and clothing. Sulfur has been used to help with respiratory problems, so perhaps a day at the baths can help cure whatever ails you.

EATS FOR KIDS The most convenient food stop is the Terme dei Papi's **snack bar and restaurant.** Alternatively, a 20-minute drive brings you to the beautiful hill town of Tuscania and the **Locanda Mirandolina** (Via del Pozzo Bianco 40/42, tel. 07/61.43.65.95), whose strengths are its outdoor dining terrace and the outstanding cooking and hospitality of Anna Maria and Carlo. If you like the experience well enough, you can rent an inexpensive room here and go back to the baths the next day.

TERME DI DIOCLEZIANO

I f you have time to visit only one bath complex in Rome, make it the Terme di Diocleziano (Baths of Diocletian). Covering over 2½ acres, it was the largest bath complex ever built in Rome, accommodating twice as many people (over 3,000 bathers daily) as the baths of Caracalla. Although much less well-preserved and -known than Caracalla, these baths are home to two recently reopened and restored museums as well as a church and cloister designed by Michelangelo. Both museums and the church are worth visiting.

Start your kids out in the baths to see its structure and the famous Aula Ottogona (Octagonal Hall), which in recent times has served as a planetarium (from 1928), a movie theater, and even a gym. The vast space of the Aula Ottogona is now an exhibition hall for larger-than-life ancient bronze statues as well as marble busts and torsos. The statue of the seated boxer tends to fascinate kids who look carefully. Can you tell the boxer's

EATS FOR KIDS The neighborhood is full of bars and restaurants—some more touristy than others—that service Termini train station passengers. The **Trattoria Elettra** (Via Principe Amedeo 72, tel. 06/474.53.97) welcomes families with a big menu, or check suggestions under Palazzo Massimo, across from this museum.

HEY, KIDS! In ancient times people regularly used public baths. Even rich folks with baths at home visited them—for company, to hear a lecture, or for the gyms—bringing servants to help them change, work out, and scrub down. In all, people could stay a whole or half day. Some emperors, like Commodus, took several baths daily. His typical routine included changing into exercise clothing, working out, sweating in a *laconicum* (sauna), dunking in a hot pool, and going to a *tepidarium* (warm room). He probably finished with a swim in a large unheated outdoor pool before heading back to the office.

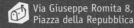 Via Giuseppe Romita 8,
Piazza della Repubblica

 06/487.06.90

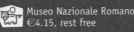 Museo Nazionale Romano
€4.15, rest free

 T–Su 9–7:45

 8 and up

age? Was he injured in his last fight? Note how brutally accurate the artist was in depicting cuts, a broken nose, a swollen eye. You can feel the gravity and fatigue in his pose.

Had your fill of statuary? Get back to checking out the bath structure itself. Walk through the archaeological remains around and beneath the Aula Ottogona to get a sense of how the structure was built (concrete poured into a brick-lined shell). Pick up the guidebook at the entrance, so you can follow the map of the original structure.

If energy allows, see the rest of the bath real estate by taking the kids around the block to the Museo Nazionale Romano (Viale Enrico de Nicola 79, tel. 06/481.55.76). The other museum at the baths has a wonderful collection of inscriptions, books of curses against gladiators, sculpture, and access to Michelangelo's cloister.

KEEP IN MIND For a terrific bargain for the family interested in seeing the best of ancient Rome, ask for the five-day combination ticket €15.50 when you enter. It covers admission to both museums here as well as the Colosseo, the Crypta Balbi (a medieval museum set within the old imperial Roman theater of Balbus), the Palatino's museum, Palazzo Altemps, Palazzo Massimo alle Terme, and other museums. All the above museums have been recently restored, and many are described in this book.

TIME ELEVATOR ROMA

"**H**istory has never been more fun," reads an advertisement for this unusual entertainment. "All it takes is an incredible trip in a Time Elevator, and Rome will never seem the same again."

So what exactly is the Time Elevator? It's a multimedia experience that teaches the legends and lore of Rome, from its founding in the 8th century BC through today.

The fun begins with four progressively difficult rounds of a Jeopardy!-style quiz on Rome, which you can play while you wait for previous elevator occupants to clear out of the theater. When the coast is clear, you are escorted into what looks like a movie theater with roller coaster seats. A safety bar drops, lights dim, and off you go to the founding of Rome with Romulus and Remus. Chased by wolves, you dip back into a time tunnel, which deposits you on the Ides of March in time to see Julius Caesar assassinated in front of your eyes. On to the Roman Empire, the arrival of Christianity, and the bloodbaths at the Colosseo.

KEEP IN MIND Even though the Time Elevator is expensive and lasts only 45 minutes, it's worth it once. It is a terrific hot-weather destination because, unlike much of Rome, the theater is air-conditioned. The Time Elevator experience is available in English and five other languages. Depending on which periods of history or which scenes pique your kids' interest, you can plan a companion excursion to either the Fontana di Trevi, Pantheon, Altare della Patria, or Foro Romano. They're all within easy walking distance. Kids under 5 and pregnant women are not permitted, as the ride gets bumpy.

Via dei Santissimi Sant'Apostoli 20

 €10.85

06/699.00.53; www.time-elevator.it

Daily 10 AM–11 PM

5 and up

The sack of Rome and the beginning of papal powers are all described in an animated and fast-paced way, thanks to inventor Rinaldi, your guide. At one point, Dr. Rinaldi's special effects even dribble rain on you. (Other special effects will go unnamed so as not to ruin the surprise.) Through the Time Elevator you can sneak into the Cappella Sistina (Sistine Chapel) to watch Michelangelo work. Dash on to the Baroque period to witness Bernini and his fabulous fountains. The unification of Italy flies past, as do Garibaldi, Mussolini, and the Pope. In a lovely last five minutes, you are airborne over the Tevere of today.

In spite of some misleading images (Florence's statue of David appears as a fountain in a gilded room), the Time Elevator does a good job of putting events in chronological order and reconstructing old Rome. Humor, special effects, and a terrific multilingual staff make this a great 45-minute overview of Roman history.

EATS FOR KIDS
See the listings for nearby Palazzo Colonna, Fontana di Trevi, and the Museo Nazionale della Pasta Alimentare. Or hop over to **Quirino** (Via delle Muratte 84, tel. 06/679.41.08) for good Roman cooking in an old-fashioned trattoria setting.

HEY, KIDS! Can you pick out some of the Time Elevator's errors? How about the scene depicting Michelangelo at work? Documents all say that he dismissed his assistants when he began work on the Sistine Chapel, so he could complete everything by himself. Yet the Time Elevator shows an assistant, brush in hand. In truth, Michelangelo would not have permitted anyone else to touch the Sistine ceiling.

TRASTEVERE

Trastevere is Rome's Left Bank. Dotted with beautiful churches, cobblestone streets, and medieval buildings, this bohemian neighborhood is like a stage set of what you thought Italy was like. Set out on foot to see the area's narrow backstreets and alleys, which take you far from the whir of *motorini* (motor scooters) to small nooks dotted with shops, fountains, family-run restaurants, small ochre-colored buildings, churches with beautiful courtyards, and craftspeople hard at work. Duck into courtyards that interest you, light candles in churches, and watch the locals gossiping on front stoops and at bars and cafés.

Trastevere corners reveal textures and perfumes. Bakeries put forth the day's specialties, and street vendors bark their wares against a backdrop of fountains, ivy-clad buildings, and umbrella-shaded coffee bars. Grab a newspaper, take the kids and a soccer ball, and head for the most beautiful of Trastevere's piazzas: Santa Maria in Trastevere. On the day of Christ's birth, oil is said to have sprung from the ground on this site. The church here,

EATS FOR KIDS Wander around and make your own great food discoveries, or, if you're at a loss, try **Checco er Carettiere** (Via Benedetta 10/13, tel. 06/581.62.49). Though touristy, it has a fun, rustic atmosphere and great food. For pizza, try **Taberna Piscinula** (*see* Bocca della Verità).

HEY, KIDS! The Trasteverini consider themselves the "Real Romans," and every summer since the 1500s they've held La Festa di Noantri (Our Own Party) in honor of the Madonna del Carmine. Similar to an enormous block party, it's a celebration with food, entertainment, and special events—not to mention streets filled with Trasteverini night and day. On the first Saturday after July 16, a statue of the Virgin covered in jewels is paraded through the streets. For about two weeks after that, the neighborhood sponsors street theater, exhibits, book sales, and kids' games. Everyone is welcome, even those who aren't *real* Romans.

West side of Tevere, from Porta Portese to Piazza delle Rovere and Viale delle Mura Aurelie

 06/583.34.57
Tourist Information Point

 Free

Daily 24 hrs

5 and up

dedicated to the Virgin Mary, contains Byzantine mosaics and Cavallini's mosaics of the life of the Virgin, both in the main apse.

Avoid the modern Viale Trastevere, where the din of traffic is overwhelming. Head instead for the smaller roadways, to discover the neighborhood's true nature. There's an open-air market at Piazza San Cosimato. Wander south of Viale Trastevere to the less-well-known *l'altro Trastevere* (the other Trastevere). On Tuesday and Thursday from 3 to 5, you can get into the oasis-like cloister of San Giovanni Battista dei Genovesi (Via Anicia 12).

Everywhere you go you find grape arbors, wisteria-choked facades, and crawling jasmine plants spanning entire courtyards. Check out the churches of Santa Cecilia and San Francesco a Ripa, each in its self-named piazza. Via della VII Coorte takes you past Rome's oldest firehouse and several of its best cobblers and bakers. Trasteverini have the reputation of being Rome's most close-knit neighbors, but kids are a real passport and you'll find folks quite welcoming.

KEEP IN MIND This is an urban walk best punctuated with frequent stops for ice cream or pizza or with browsing at newsstands or shops. Combine a neighborhood walk with a visit to the Orto Botanico (*see* #30) or the Porta Portese flea market (*see* #19), which sets up here every Sunday morning. At Trastevere Games (Piazza Mastai 1, tel. 06/581.98.70), kids 10 and up can play a wide assortment of video games and pinball, but be warned: It's a smoke-filled den.

VIA APPIA ANTICA

On Sundays, one of Rome's most important roads, the Via Appia Antica (Appian Way), closes to traffic and opens itself up for family exploration. Begun in 312 BC by magistrate Appius Claudius, this cypress-lined thoroughfare with 11 miles of stone pavement becomes a great, albeit bumpy, place to ride bikes. So don those helmets and head for the Porta di San Sebastiano. You can pedal as far as you wish, but cover at least the first 2 miles to get a sense of this extraordinary marriage of road, buildings, and verdant national park.

Without cars careening past, you can enjoy the scenery. Ivy-covered stone walls yield to green fields, tombs, and monuments. You'll pedal under an overpass, over a bridge, past houses and column bits. As you set out, keep your eyes open on the left for the crossroad of Via Ardeatina and the church of Santa Maria in Palmis. According to legend, St. Peter met Jesus here. Leave your bikes at the church's entrance and check out the marble slab with footprints on it. Some people feel they were left by Christ when he was chatting with St. Peter, but scholars think they simply marked a blessing place for travelers.

KEEP IN MIND Some cars manage to drive the Via Appia Antica even when it's closed to traffic. If you're biking, stay alert and keep to the side of the road to allow renegade cars to pass. An ideal start to your tour is to visit the Museo delle Mura di Roma (*see* #38) at Porta San Sebastiano. And if you're not up for cycling, consider the Archeobus (*see* #67) for transportation.

Suggested stretch: Porta di
San Sebastiano to Via di Cecilia Metella

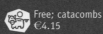
Free; catacombs
€4.15

Daily 24 hrs, but biking suggested Su;
catacombs daily 8:30–12 and 2:30–5

06/77.20.35.35 Tourist Information
Point; www.parcoappiaantica.org

All ages

At the Catacombe di San Callisto (Via Appia Antica 110, tel. 06/51.30.15.80), you can see four layers of tombs, tunnels, and the burial places of several popes and martyrs. A flashlight comes in handy, as passageways are not well lit. Stick with your group (tours are given by priests) as you don't want to get lost in this labyrinth of mossy, damp passageways. A bit farther on, the Catacombe di San Sebastiano (Via Appia Antica 136, tel. 06/51.30.15.80) contains more-pillaged tombs with compelling early Christian graffiti (crudely carved doves with olive branches in their beaks) and dark, dank passages still sealed off from the public.

You can choose to have lunch in a grand country-style restaurant or picnic, but however you spend your time, you'll be seeing one of the most evocative stretches of road in the world.

HEY, KIDS! You may have heard that early Christians hid from their persecutors in the catacombs. But most research indicates that the catacombs were purely places of burial and burial services, not places of secret meetings and hiding.

EATS FOR KIDS It is lovely to eat lunch in the large garden area under the wisteria at the **Hostaria dell'Archeologia** (Via Appia Antica 139, tel. 06/788.04.94). For information on the Antica Roma and Cecilia Metella restaurants, see the Museo delle Mura di Roma and the Fosse Ardeatine. A picnic is another, less expensive option and a sure kid-pleaser, especially if all that biking has left you with big appetites.

VIA GIULIA

The shortest distance between two points is a straight line, right? That's the basic idea behind this 16th-century cobblestone roadway, which runs from the city center toward the Vatican. During the Renaissance, as today, Via Giulia was a vanity address, and many famous people lived here. Stroll along this avenue of secret gardens, tiny churches, shops, and perfectly proportioned Renaissance architecture; stop at interesting sights; and peer into inviting courtyards.

Start at the street's southernmost point: the big drooling Fontana Mascherone (Mask Fountain). Today this mouth spurts nonpotable water, but legend has it that it used to spout wine for special occasions. A few steps away, you'll pass under an ivy-covered overpass, an elevated pedestrian walkway begun by Michelangelo. To your right is the back of Palazzo Farnese, where you can peer through the *cancello* (gate) at the gardens. Next, on the left, is Santa Maria dell'Orazione e Morte (Via Giulia and Via dei Farnesi), whose facade is decorated with skulls and winged hourglasses to remind us of our mortality.

KEEP IN MIND If your kids have the energy, take a one-block detour from elegant Via Giulia to visit the darker side of life: the Museo Criminologico di Roma (*see* #41), Rome's criminology museum. Medieval torture instruments, guillotines, and executioners' capes provide a real contrast.

HEY, KIDS! The cobblestones you are walking on are made of basalt and are shaped like back teeth—squarish at the top and narrow at the base. Set in sand to create a natural drainage system, the stones are called *sanpietrini* (little Saint Peters). Just as the Catholic church is built on Saint Peter (Peter means "rock"), all of Rome is built on little Saint Peters. Look for the larger cobblestones measuring about 12" square. These are called *bastardone* (big bastards). You can imagine a worker naming them after lugging them about.

Fontana Mascherone to
San Giovanni dei Fiorentini

 Free

Daily 24 hrs

 06/36.00.43.99 Tourist Information
Point; www.romaturismo.com

8 and up

It was this church's responsibility to collect plague victims' bodies and give them Christian burials. Look for two marble plaques, one of a winged skeleton pointing to an inscription (in Latin)—"As you see me, you one day will be"—and the other of a plague victim collapsing in a field.

Just past the church, the Palazzo Falconieri (Via Giulia 1) sports huge spooky falcon heads on its corners. It's said Napoleon's uncle lived here. Farther on the left, the church with the beautiful dome (Sant'Eligio degli Orefici) is believed to have been designed by Raphael (1509). He probably enjoyed the short commute here from his home (Via Giulia 84/86). En route, try to pick out the building that was once a prison (Via Giulia 52). The road ends at San Giovanni dei Fiorentini, a white baroque church, on the left, where animals are welcome as part of the congregation. By the time you've reached it, you'll hopefully have peeked into gateways, courtyards, gardens, galleries, and gift shops and caught a glimpse of this road's lovely spoils.

EATS FOR KIDS For a nice change of pace, **Le Piramidi** (Vicolo del Gallo 11, tel. 06/678.90.61) is a favorite for Arab and Egyptian food. Mimmo will wrap your pita bread sandwich in paper for easy eating while walking. **Ditirambo** (Piazza della Cancelleria 74, tel. 06/687.16.26) has excellent food, including sorbet-filled fruits for dessert. It's closed Mondays. **Taverna Giulia** (Vicolo dell'Oro 23, tel. 06/686.97.68) is a slightly fancier stop for Ligurian food, and Campo dei Fiori (see #61) is also just steps away, a great food destination come lunchtime.

VILLA BORGHESE

To get away from the city and its traffic, you need go no farther than the Villa Borghese. Not what Americans think of as a "villa"—except in the sense that it was the estate of the Borghese family before it was taken over by the government in 1902—this huge, somewhat overgrown 17th-century park extends for over 4 miles through the heart of Rome's city center.

Dotting the extensive property are a number of museums (*see* the Museo Borghese and Villa Giulia), which warrant a visit. However, even if you never darken a museum doorway, you will chance upon dozens of worthwhile discoveries, including fountains, paths, and a little artificial lake where you can rent rowboats or feed ducks your breakfast scraps. You can picnic, take a bicycle ride, or simply stroll, and even on the hottest summer days, shade trees (palms, huge umbrella pines, elms, chestnuts, cypress, and fruit trees, including banana and plantain) provide shelter from the midday sun.

KEEP IN MIND Bike rentals are available at the Muro Torto and Porta Pinciana entrances to the park. Prices vary depending on the season but are very reasonable. You may be asked to leave a license or passport as security until your bike is returned. The bikes are generally well maintained, and the rental fee includes a chain and lock. Also see the listing for Autobus 116, a great way to get to the park.

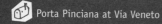 Porta Pinciana at Via Veneto

 Free

Daily 24 hrs

06/68.13.60.61
Tourist Information Point

All ages

Enter the park from the Porta Pinciana at the top of Via Veneto. From here you can walk down long shaded avenues to an aviary, temples (not old by Roman standards), flower beds, and statuary honoring heros of Rome's illustrious past. Kids often like to visit the hippodrome (called Piazza di Siena), a huge grassy area bordered by shade trees, where horse shows are held each May. If you get tired of walking, take the little trolley train €1.05–€1.55, depending on the length of your ride), which makes stops throughout the garden, including at the zoo. The zoo itself is rather dated compared to most other city zoos worldwide but is being improved as of this writing.

Don't forget to bring your camera. The park and its wonderful statuary, vast garden beds and greenery, amphitheater, and the entry to the Galappatoio (a horseback riding school) make ideal backdrops for family photos—so you can remember this respite long after you've returned to the hustle and bustle of the city.

HEY, KIDS! Look for the old-fashioned carousel nestled in the middle of the park. It's next to the Teatro dei Piccoli, a vintage theater that shows movies and cartoons for kids, another great escape from the summer heat.

EATS FOR KIDS Avoid the overpriced food carts and drink trucks within the park. Instead shop for a picnic before you come and then stop anywhere in the park when you get hungry or thirsty. Keep an eye open for *fontanelle,* which provide cool drinkable water. Alternatively, walk down Via Veneto to the **Hard Rock Cafe** (Via Veneto 62A, tel. 06/420.30.51) and its restaurant, bar, boutique, and rock memorabilia.

VILLA D'ESTE

I n 1550 Cardinnale Ippolito II d'Este redecorated a Benedictine monastery and turned it into a villa with nicely frescoed rooms, many of which you can visit. But the real lure here is the extensive gardens, resembling a Renaissance version of a water park.

If your kids can be slowed enough to set foot in the villa, show them the Sala della Caccia (Room of the Hunt), with its frescoes of wild game, ships, and shipwrecks. Exit onto the back staircase, which leads to a terrific view and gardens that slope away from you. The best way to view the garden, however, is from the bottom of the hill, which is how 16th-century guests would have arrived. Kids love running pell-mell down the hill and then retracing their steps or trying new paths to get back to the villa. Urge them to stop along the way, though, to take in the statuary and other interesting sights.

It is amazing how many different ways water is presented here. It flows, it dribbles, it squirts, it sprays, it drips, it rushes, it gurgles. Water jets 30 and 40 feet into the air

EATS FOR KIDS A **bar** on the premises serves basic food and drink. Otherwise, try **Del Falcone** (Via Trevio 34, tel. 07/ 74.31.23.58), with excellent food at reasonable prices, or pack a picnic to eat on the grounds of the Villa Gregoriana.

HEY, KIDS! If you were a dinner guest here in 1550, first you'd have to get to the villa's main entrance, and to do that you'd have to make your way up the hill. Over and over, you'd have to choose whether to turn left or right, and one direction was always steeper than the other. Adding to the "fun" were spouts of water here and there that would be set off by your footsteps. It's thought that there were more water hazards on the less steep stretches, so guests tended to arrive at the house breathless (the braver climbers) or wet (the lazier strollers).

in some places and pours into moss- and fern-lined fish ponds in others. The garden resonates with the sound of all that water. There's a banister with a channel of flowing water, a fountain that at one time made sounds like screech owls and songbirds, and, though it is not working now, an amazing water organ that used to play music as guests arrived. (Sound was made by jets of water forced through different sized spigots at different speeds.) Look also for a carved stone version of the she-wolf with Romulus and Remus and la Rometta (Little Rome), which has miniatures of all the great monuments of Rome.

Walkways frequently force you to choose between two paths rather than leading directly to the villa's entrance. Meandering is part of the experience. So take your time and your camera, and enjoy the mist-cooled air and occasional rainbows provided by these waterworks.

KEEP IN MIND Though it's tempting to do so, you're not allowed to drink any of the water (it's not potable anyway), play with the water displays, or picnic on the premises. Reward your kids' restraint by taking them to the Villa Gregoriana (entrance at Porta Sant'Angelo), a beautiful natural park ideal for hiking, horsing around, picnicking, and exploring. Its main path leads to wonderful waterfalls and a grotto. Or combine the Villa d'Este with a visit and picnic at Villa Adriana (Via Tiburtina, tel. 0774/53.02.03).

VILLA DORIA PAMPHILI

4

Rome's largest park sprawls across much of Rome's Monteverde neighborhood. Major roadways have been cut through her lush green expanse, but it is still possible to feel far away from people in this extensive oasis.

Enter through the main gate with its grand triumphal arch, but once past it, the garden's formality ends. Unlike other parks with perfectly manicured shrubbery or intimate, measurable spaces, Doria Pamphili spreads before you in an attractive state of disorder. It is a great destination for the adventuresome hiker, biker, walker, jogger, or explorer in your family. Dirt pathways lead through over 400 acres, past grove after grove of umbrella pine trees, abandoned buildings, artificial lakes, grassy spots, stretches of gravel and pebbles, a chapel, soccer fields, and the villa itself. Keep walking through nature's lovely randomness and you will come to sandboxes, swings, and slides—okay for the younger crowd but seemingly minute and tame compared to the groves of trees beckoning to you.

KEEP IN MIND You can book a tour of the Casino del Bel Respiro, nestled by the western walls of the park, by contacting the Associazione Citta Nascosta (tel. 06/331.60.59). Closed to the public except by appointment, the house is used for official diplomatic gatherings of the Italian government and its guests. The beautiful boxwood gardens inspired by French formal gardens are definitely worth a visit.

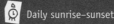
Kids can join pick-up soccer games, throw a baseball, walk the dog, or meet friends for a picnic. Older kids are usually happy to have nothing structured to do except unleash their energies on the wide open spaces. There are trees to climb, playing fields, clearings, and limitless paths to explore, and the park is one of the few great places in Rome to fly kites.

The park was developed by the Pamphili family between 1640 and 1664. It originally had a system of canals, fountains, and three artificial waterfalls that cascaded into a lake. Purchased by the Italian government in 1957, the Villa Doria Pamphili became a public park in 1965. Many of its buildings are still being reconstructed, but the grounds are abundant and totally accessible.

HEY, KIDS! A little lake here is inhabited by nutria, mammals that originated in South America but somehow ended up here. Resembling large rats with segmented tails and coarse fur, they waddle out of the lake to chow down on a banquet of (hopefully healthy) leftovers

EATS FOR KIDS Kids are welcomed like kings and queens at **Il Vascello** (Via G. Massari 8/10, tel. 06/580.65.17), and in good weather you can eat on the terrace with all the other families. For other restaurants, see listings for Villa Sciarra and Piazzale Garibaldi, but the most fun is to picnic and let the kids run around.

VILLA FARNESINA

In the 1500s, a wealthy Siennese banker, Alessandro Chigi, moved his family and financial operations to Rome. With the guidance of architect Baldasarre Peruzzi, he built a magnificent riverside residence in Trastevere, where he held famously extravagant parties. Writings document exotic menu items such as parrot tongue sauce, and silver and gold serving dishes were supposedly dramatically thrown into the Tevere in front of guests. (Servants had earlier placed nets so they could be fished out again when the party was over.)

Today the villa makes a great stop with kids because the house is neither huge nor exhausting. It has beautifully painted rooms and perspective puzzles to figure out and is conveniently located next to the Orto Botanico (Botanical Gardens), where kids can blow off steam afterwards.

EATS FOR KIDS A picnic in the Orto Botanico makes for a great afternoon. Also see restaurants under Orto Botanico and Museo Sanitario, or try **Otello Hostaria Pizzeria** (Piazza S. Egidio 53, tel. 06/589.68.48) for Roman specialties and grilled meats, fresh fish, and pizza.

In the first room, Raphael's famous *Galatea* shows her in a paddle-propelled seashell being dragged out to sea by two dolphins. But the stunning panel is just one of the

HEY, KIDS! Try solving another perspective puzzle upstairs in the Salone delle Prospettive (Perspective Room)—by Peruzzi again—by finding the one place where everything looks right. Perspective is a way of representing depth and space on a flat surface. This is done by painting some objects smaller than others and by having parallel lines converge. Perspective as a mathematical system was invented by an Italian (Brunelleschi) in the 1500s. While you're here, check out the early graffiti on these frescoes. They were left as a historic document when the frescoes were restored. What's the earliest date you can find?

beautiful frescoes in the room. Overhead an astrological painting depicts exactly where the planets and stars were at the moment of Chigi's birth. Lunettes painted by Sebastiano di Piombo show scenes of gods and goddesses. The large drawing of a man's head in the final lunette is believed to be by the architect, Peruzzi.

Exit this room for the loggia. The ceiling, designed by Raphael, looks like a huge garden bower to which are tied tapestry-like paintings of the marriage of Cupid and Psyche and of Mount Olympus, with gods and goddesses cavorting about. The scenes are bedecked with every fruit and vegetable imaginable, from turnips to pomegranates to grapes, squash, melons, and even cauliflower. Birds, bats, butterflies, hawks, and gulls sweep in and out of the picture plane. It is a feast of bounty and abundance. Can you find the one point in the room where you can keep all the perspective straight? Figuring out perspective was a Renaissance fascination, and it makes looking at the art here interesting and fun today.

KEEP IN MIND The Gabinetto Nazionale delle Stampe (National Print and Drawing Collection) is housed in the building and sponsors the occasional exhibition of items from its extensive collection. If there is a show, don't miss it. Not only is the collection worthwhile, but the exhibition space is a suite of several beautifully decorated rooms otherwise closed to the public. The restoration of the upstairs bedroom, painted by Sodoma of Alexander the Great and his wife's (Roxanne's) wedding night, was recently completed and will appeal to any romantics in your family.

VILLA GIULIA

It's a shame you can't arrive here the way Pope Julius III did, via a boat festooned with flowers, but a walk through the Villa Borghese isn't a bad way to arrive either. However you arrive, once here you won't be disappointed by either the building or the collection.

All the important architects of the day, including Vignola and Michelangelo, were called in to build this countryside retreat. Its plain facade belies the beautiful Renaissance marriage of house and garden, and the villa's two frescoed arms seem to embrace its surroundings. Inside is the world's most complete collection of Etruscan art. The Etruscans, who predated the Romans, believed in an afterlife, and objects from their tombs and necropoli (cities of the dead) tell us much about them. However, much is still shrouded in mystery. Were they indigenous to the area? Did they come from Asia Minor? Their enigmatic language has yet to be completely deciphered (see the second-floor exhibit), and their fascination with pattern and decoration is seductive. Here are mirror backs that inspired Picasso's etchings and elongated figures that look like Giacometti's work.

HEY, KIDS! Can you imagine being buried with a chariot and two horses? Throw in some armor, swords, shields, and spears and you've got to have a pretty big tomb. Whole families were often buried in different chambers of the same structure, along with their servants, pets, and all the above equipment. Check out the wall charts showing some of these multichambered tombs to get an idea of just how big they were.

Piazzale Villa Giulia 9

 €4.15

T–Sa 9–7, Su 9–2

06/322.65.71, 06/841.64.00
guided tours in English

10 and up

Remind the kids that these artifacts—related to war, farming, jewelry, and transportation—were packed into graves over 2,000 years ago so the dead could use them in the afterlife. Avoid the long rooms of pots and vases unless your child is into cartooning, since the depictions of gods and goddesses are first-rate inspiration for superhero drawings. Don't miss the famous terra-cotta sarcophagus from Cerveteri, depicting a married couple at a banquet. This more than any other object here reveals the equal position women held in Etruscan society. The exquisite jewelry collection presents originals and contemporary copies.

If your children get overwhelmed, suggest the computer stations (second floor) with English descriptions, or wander through the gardens to the museum's snack bar, with wicker chairs and immense windows. The gardens have a lovely *nymphaeum* as well as a reproduction of what an Etruscan temple may have looked like.

EATS FOR KIDS

The museum's **snack bar,** in the rear of the garden, is fine for sandwiches and light fare, but the **Caffè delle Arti** (Via Gramsci 73, tel. 06/32.41.52), in the museum of modern art next door, has better lunch selections and a terrific terrace.

KEEP IN MIND Villa Giulia is a great preface or follow-up to a day trip to Cerveteri (*see* #56) or Tarquinia, Etruscan hill towns to the north of Rome. Today you can still see the actual tombs that a lot of these relics came from. Cerveteri's tombs are described in this book, while Tarquinia and its amazing painted tombs are just a bit farther north. In both places you can still enter the necropoli and wander about with your amateur archaeologists.

VILLA SCIARRA

For younger children, there is no more beautiful Roman park than Villa Sciarra and no more ideal place to play than its small, varied, but confined spaces. Leaving the bustle of Rome behind, you enter through a gateway into another world, almost a *Secret Garden* experience. A little gravel-lined piazza flanked by a limestone fountain is to your right, and an enormous bird and animal cage is to your left. Here your family can feed rabbits, ducks, and geese through the caging, sit in the sunshine, picnic, or read a book as well as use the slides, swings, sandboxes, and climbing apparatus. Little ones like the spiral topiary, gazebos, a small carousel, and an itsy-bitsy roller coaster.

If you look as far back as Roman times, Villa Sciarra was supposedly the hangout of a wood nymph. In more recent history (1902), the villa was purchased by the American diplomat George Wurst and his wife, Henriette Tower. Together they rekindled the villa's glorious past, restoring the buildings and gardens, entertaining visiting VIPs, and raising rare birds and plants, which were occasionally cooked up in the kitchens for guests.

HEY, KIDS!

This is a great place to unload leftover toast or wilting lettuce. Bring grains or vegetables for the inhabitants of the bird cage, and make instant friends. You may find baby chicks, ducks, or a rabbit (or two, three, or four!) depending on when you visit.

KEEP IN MIND Safety is a parent-controlled issue in Italy. By American standards, you may find swings placed too closely together or too near a walkway. Initially, you may have to be more involved in your children's play than you're used to until you work out limitations and caution areas. But this is an ideal park to foster international friendships among wee ones. By the way, the theme of the park's statuary is the eternal battle between Vice and Virtue.

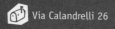

These days lots of au pairs, nannies, doting grandparents, and attentive families from the neighborhood cluster here, reading newspapers, strolling, and comparing baby facts and fictions. Newborns from nearby Ospedale Salvator Mundi (Salvator Mundi Hospital) are often treated to their first fresh air in this park. In springtime, older kids collect guppies (from the fountain basin) and butterflies here, while spotted lizards dash to escape their grasp. But generally, older kids become frustrated by the lack of wide open spaces for kicking a soccer ball or running freely. Nearby Villa Doria Pamphili (*see* #4) is a better choice for those who need more room.

Flower beds and little reflecting pools surround the many limestone statues, which, by the way, are all unified by a theme: a famous duality. Can you guess what it is?

EATS FOR KIDS Via Carini and its continuation, Via Barille, have lots of pastry shops and sandwich bars, the best of which is **Pasticceria Cristiani** (Via Barille 68, tel. 06/589.77.09), by the Catholic church. If you are a dark chocolate, whipped cream, and puff pastry lover, get the profiterole. For lunch, **Il Cortile** (Via Cavalloti 46, tel. 06/580.34.33) has indoor and outdoor seating, some of the best grilled fish and meat in Rome, and a fantastic antipasto table.

CLASSIC GAMES

"I SEE SOMETHING YOU DON'T SEE AND IT IS BLUE." Stuck for a way to get your youngsters to settle down in a museum? Sit them down on a bench in the middle of a room and play this vintage favorite. The leader gives just one clue—the color—and everybody guesses away.

"I'M GOING TO THE GROCERY..." The first player begins, "I'm going to the grocery and I'm going to buy... " and finishes the sentence with the name of an object, found in grocery stores, that begins with the letter "A." The second player repeats what the first player has said, and adds the name of another item that starts with "B." The third player repeats everything that has been said so far and adds something that begins with "C" and so on through the alphabet. Anyone who skips or misremembers an item is out (or decide up front that you'll give hints to all who need 'em). You can modify the theme depending on where you're going that day, as "I'm going to X and I'm going to see..."

FAMILY ARK Noah had his ark—here's your chance to build your own. It's easy: Just start naming animals and work your way through the alphabet, from antelope to zebra.

PLAY WHILE YOU WAIT

NOT THE GOOFY GAME Have one child name a category. (Some ideas: first names, last names, animals, countries, friends, feelings, foods, hot or cold things, clothing.) Then take turns naming things that fall into that category. You're out if you name something that doesn't belong in the category—or if you can't think of another item to name. When only one person remains, start again. Choose categories depending on where you're going or where you've been—historic topics if you've seen a historic sight, animal topics before or after the zoo, upside-down things if you've been to the circus, and so on. Make the game harder by choosing category items in A-B-C order.

DRUTHERS How do your kids really feel about things? Just ask. "Would you rather eat worms or hamburgers? Hamburgers or candy?" Choose serious and silly topics—and have fun!

BUILD A STORY "Once upon a time there lived..." Finish the sentence and ask the rest of your family, one at a time, to add another sentence or two. Bring a tape recorder along to record the narrative—and you can enjoy your creation again and again.

GOOD TIMES GALORE

WIGGLE & GIGGLE Give your kids a chance to stick out their tongues at you. Start by making a face, then have the next person imitate you and add a gesture of his own—snapping fingers, winking, clapping, sneezing, or the like. The next person mimics the first two and adds a third gesture, and so on.

JUNIOR OPERA During a designated period of time, have your kids sing everything they want to say.

THE QUIET GAME Need a good giggle—or a moment of calm to figure out your route? The driver sets a time limit and everybody must be silent. The last person to make a sound wins.

HIGH FIVES

TOP FIVE
Il Pantheon
Stanze di Sant'Ignazio
Altare della Patria
Terme dei Papi
Orto Botanico

BEST OUTDOORS
Sperlonga

BEST CULTURAL ACTIVITY
Fosse Ardeatine

BEST MUSEUM
Casina delle Civette

WACKIEST
Museo Sanitario

NEW & NOTEWORTHY
Time Elevator Roma

SOMETHING FOR EVERYONE

ALL AROUND TOWN

ALL AROUND TOWN